PRAISE FOR *DARING TO BE*

'You can't help but be captivated by this book, from the story of its discovery through the weave of its emotions. I felt as though I had been trusted with a deeply personal history.'

James Hawes, director of *One Life* and *The Amateur*

'Immaculately researched and beautifully written. Treading in Inge and Kitty's footsteps feels as fresh and precarious as it was when they fled the Nazis.'

Malcolm Brabant, journalist and co-author of *The Daughter of Auschwitz*

'A compelling read told with pace and skill.'

Mark Blackaby, author and winner of the Betty Trask Prize for *You'll Never be Here Again*

'This book provides a vivid and intimate portrait of the consequences of irrational hatred and its eventual defeat.'

David Rose, investigations editor of *UnHerd*

'Gripping. A horrifying account of the creeping terror that was the life of every German Jew under Hitler's evil regime. Helen John has used relatives' papers and diaries to recount her own family's descent from the top echelons of German society to becoming non-persons. A timely reminder of how individual acts of antisemitism can poison the minds of an entire nation.'

Michael Smith, bestselling author of *Foley: The Spy Who Saved 10,000 Jews*

'*Daring to Be* is both an intimate family portrait and a powerful testament to the far-reaching consequences of persecution. Helen John writes with clarity and compassion, ensuring that her mother's story - and the voices of so many others like her - are not lost to history. A compelling, beautifully crafted work, this book is a vital addition to the literature of Jewish exile and survival.'

                Dr Joseph Cronin, director of Leo Baeck Institute, London

'This book provides a deeply impressive testimony to the resilience of young refugees who escaped the Nazi terror in the 1930s. Lucidly written, it balances masterly anecdotes with observations on the German regime that pushed millions of people into the abyss. I highly recommend this small yet immensely rich book.'

                Professor Andreas W. Daum, State University of New York and editor of *The Second Generation: Émigrés from Nazi Germany as Historians*

'A richly illustrated narrative that is vivid and deeply moving.'
                Professor Dr Ernst Müller, Humboldt University, Berlin

'A poignant history of Europe in the 1930s, beautifully expressed through the diaries of one family.'

                Lord Alf Dubs, Kindertransport refugee and member of the House of Lords

DARING TO BE

Inge and Kitty's Escape from Nazi Germany

HELEN JOHN

First published in Great Britain in 2025 by
Helen John, in partnership with Whitefox Publishing Ltd

www.wearewhitefox.com

Copyright © Helen John, 2025

ISBN 978-1-917523-12-7
Also available as an eBook
ISBN 978-1-917523-13-4

Helen John asserts the moral right to be
identified as the author of this work.

All rights reserved. No part of this publication may
be reproduced, stored in a retrieval system or transmitted
in any form or by any means, electronic, mechanical,
photocopying, recording or otherwise, without
prior written permission of the author.

While every effort has been made to trace the owners of
copyright material reproduced herein, the author would like to
apologise for any omissions and will be pleased to incorporate
missing acknowledgements in any future editions.

All photographs and illustrations in this book
© Helen John, unless otherwise stated.

Designed and typeset by seagulls.net
Cover design by Jet Purdie
Project management by Whitefox Publishing Ltd

*To our brave and wonderful mothers
- Inge and Kitty, and to Oscar,
the grandfather I heard so much
about but never met.*

AUTHOR'S NOTE

Throughout the book, I have quoted from both Inge and Kitty's diaries extensively. There are also quotes from numerous letters and accounts from family members looking back at events subsequently. I have tried to make it clear throughout which quotes are contemporaneous and which are with the benefit of hindsight.

The Reichsmark (RM) was the German currency from 1924 to 1945. Conversions from Reichsmarks are calculated at 1,000RM = £80 during World War II, with £1 in 1939 being worth around £83.50 in 2025. Calculations are difficult due to the fluctuating currency rates at the time.

PROLOGUE

MUM AND ME

My mother, Kitty, died at her home in north-west London in August 2023, just a few months shy of her hundredth birthday. Clearing out her four-bedroom house was a sad task for me, her only daughter. My father, Ernest, had died a few years before.

I was several days into sorting through drawers, files and boxes of old newspapers and letters, when I reached an ill-fitting cupboard on top of the wardrobe in the guest bedroom. The air by now was full of dust and my hands were black and sticky from old newsprint.

At the back of the cupboard were two shoeboxes adorned with photos of old-fashioned women's shoes. Inside were an assortment of four handwritten books of different shapes and sizes. One was leatherbound with a small, open padlock, others were fabric-bound notebooks. They were Mum's diaries covering the period from 1938, when she was fifteen years old, to 1945, when she was twenty-one. Every inch was covered with writing, some pages neat and on some, her script was frantic-looking with the pen pressed hard against the page. There were photos and newspaper cuttings stuck to some of the entries.

An accompanying Sainsbury's bag contained three 6x4-inch photo albums with miniature black-and-white photos, each the size of a postage stamp, and two small sketchbooks. Holding up a magnifying glass I could see images of young Kitty and her sister, Inge, that I had never seen before. Some were happy family snaps, but others were more chilling. One depicted her fellow pupils on a school trip raising their arms in a Nazi salute.

There were also three autograph books with a photo of a smiling girl on each page and a short poem, presumably by each of them. These were Mum's classmates – from her German school, from her Jewish school and then from her school in Scotland. I knew nothing about the diaries, photos or books and to me, they amounted to historical treasures.

I was hopeful they would help me fill in the blanks about my mother's life. I had always known that she was of Jewish descent, that her family suffered under the Nazis and were incredibly fortunate to escape to the UK, but there were few details. Everything Mum told me was through the lens of the present - that everything worked out okay - and, consequently, the Nazi persecution and my family's subsequent escape to the UK were relayed as minor footnotes. Diaries, on the other hand, are contemporaneous - would they give me an insight into what really happened and how it felt to be fifteen and scared?

Days later, underneath gardening tools in my parents' garage, I came across an old suitcase the size of a carry-on holdall. There were stickers from the ship SS *Bremen* for the journey from Bremerhaven on Germany's north-east coast to Southampton. It was my mother's 'freedom suitcase', containing all her worldly possessions when she had left Berlin in August 1939.

MUM'S 'FREEDOM SUITCASE'

Why hadn't Mum ever shown me any of this? I had studied history at university, I am nosey and a journalist - I would have been fascinated. My aunt, Inge, often mentioned the diaries she had written during the 1930s and '40s but Mum had never mentioned hers.

My mother and I had always been close. While we sometimes quarrelled over her risk-averseness, she was

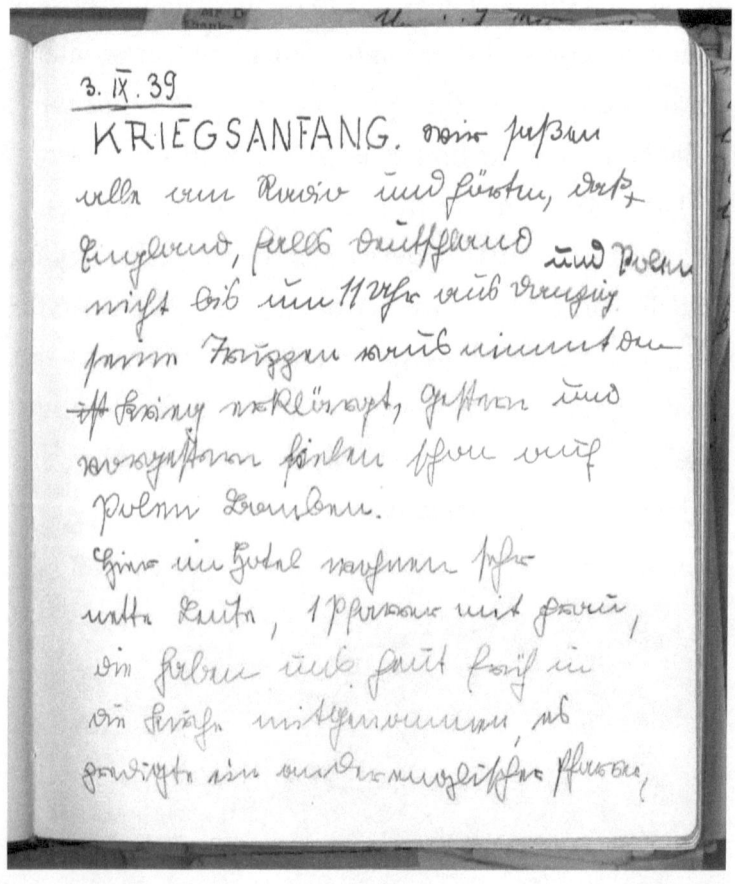

KITTY'S DIARY

the kindest and most considerate person I have ever known. She was also quietly determined and highly intelligent with a gentle, unassuming nature.

My excitement on handling Mum's precious diaries was followed by crushing disappointment. The diaries were indecipherable. Both my mum and Inge had been taught to write in elaborate Sütterlin; German script.

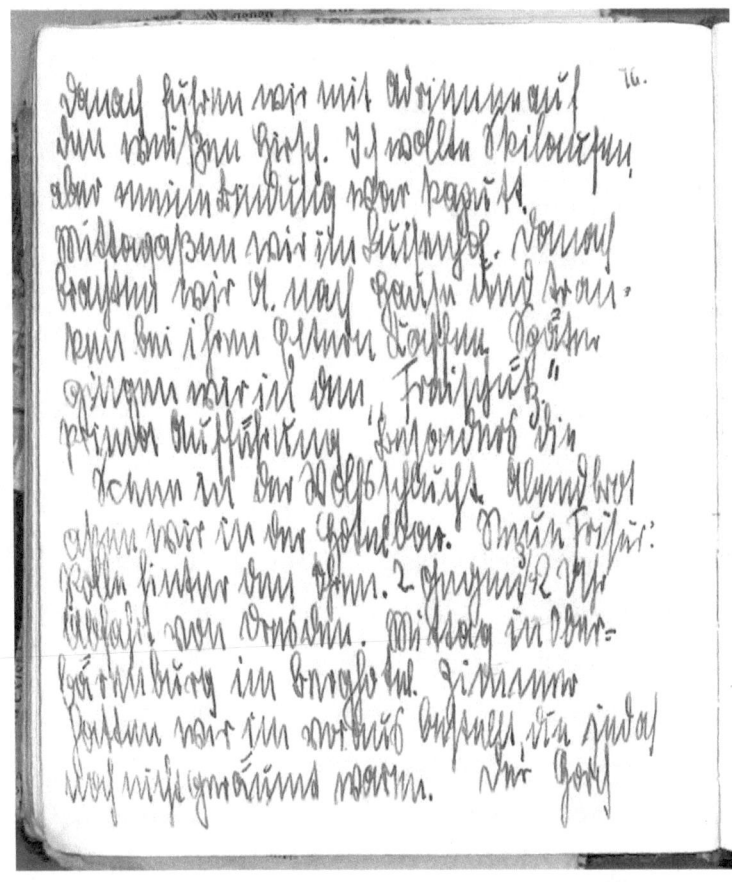

INGE'S DIARY

This Gothic font designed by the graphic artist Ludwig Sütterlin was taught in German schools from 1920 and at the time was seen as sophisticated and modern. It was subsequently banned by the Nazis in 1941, who declared it to be Judenlettern (Jewish letters) and replaced it with Latin-type letters such as Antiqua.

It was so frustrating.

I contacted the Wiener Holocaust Library in London who suggested I should speak to Carolin Sommer, who is not only an expert German-English translator but one of the few Sütterlin transcribers in the world today.

I gave Mum's and Auntie Inge's diaries to Carolin. Within a few weeks, Carolin had unlocked the diaries by rewriting their words into modern German. While I was well-aware of the broad brushstrokes of Mum's and Inge's childhoods, I now had the fine detail not only of the facts but also of their feelings at the time.

There are stark differences in the tone of the diaries. Inge's are very factual and demonstrate outrage at the mounting indignities forced upon the family. Her sister Kitty, my mother, was younger and a little less aware of the big picture. Throughout she sounds bewildered and upset by the happenings around her.

I'll never know whether Mum actively hid the diaries or whether she simply forgot about them. I'm not convinced she could have forgotten them - she wrote pages daily during the most significant, scary and impressionable period of her life. My personal view is that reopening the diaries would have brought back many painful and unwanted feelings and maybe, since she survived, she considered them to be of no consequence. She talked about happy memories from her past - about her sister, her father and her dogs - but of the circumstances around her emigration, she spoke rarely. So while she wasn't ready to throw the diaries away, perhaps it made sense to lay them carefully in a shoebox at the back of a cupboard - in the dark and out of sight.

INTRODUCTION

KITTY WITH HER GRANDCHILDREN FREDDIE AND CLARA

'Here I am human. Here I can dare to be.'
From Goethe's *Faust*. Quoted by Inge to Kitty
on arrival in Southampton, August 1939.

Kitty was a happy person who adored her family. Her mantelpiece and shelves were filled with dozens of photographs of me when I was young and her two grandchildren, Freddie and Clara. Visitors to her house thought she must have an enormous family, which she did not.

She rejoiced in good news from friends and family and radiated positivity. Her best friend throughout her life was her older sister, Inge. Both spoke fluent English with strong German accents. Strangely enough, they never spoke German together as adults but chirruped merrily like inseparable songbirds in their distinctive and identical way. Mum never spoke German to me either. With her experiences of anti-Semitism and as an unwanted refugee in the UK, she had often felt like an outsider. She wanted me to fit in like everybody else.

Their early childhood in central Berlin had been joyful. In the photos from that time, many of which were new to me, they always look cheerful - hugging their beloved dachshunds, giggling with friends and, in Kitty's case, suspended in some gymnastic contortion. Even though their mother insisted that the girls wore identical long plaits and her home-made dresses, their appearance seemed quite different. Whereas Kitty looked dishevelled from all her physical exertions, Inge appeared serene and poised. She was always the more careful and serious of the girls. Kitty was carefree and optimistic.

Inge wrote to Kitty on her eightieth birthday: 'People don't believe us when we tell them that we never quarrelled. We were always surrounded by love until Hitler came.'

DARING TO BE

INGE AND KITTY, 1920s

INGE AND KITTY, EARLY 2000s

And when Hitler came, their lives fell apart - slowly and imperceptibly at first. Although Inge and Kitty were Lutheran, they had three Jewish grandparents and a Jewish father, and consequently became victims of the Nazi regime.

All Inge and Kitty ever wanted was to live a normal life.

CHAPTER 1

EARLY YEARS

KITTY LEFT, INGE RIGHT

Ingeborg Harriet Fehr was born in Berlin on 4 March 1922 and Kitty Lucie Alice Fehr on 16 December 1923.

Although punitive reparations from the 1919 Treaty of Versailles had brought economic hardship to Germany, the girls' privileged upbringing protected them from the harsh realities faced by many of their compatriots.

Their family was highly respected. The great, the good and the famous came to consult with their father, Professor Oscar Fehr, a world-renowned ophthalmologist.

HELEN JOHN

KITTY AND INGE AROUND 1929

KITTY WITH OSCAR, 1930   OSCAR

Oscar's success is well documented in newspaper cuttings of the era. Since 1906 he had been head physician at the department of eye diseases at the Rudolf Virchow Hospital, one of the most important eye clinics in Germany. Oscar published more than forty papers and was the first to identify swimming pool conjunctivitis, leading to the practice of adding chlorine to swimming pools. He worked from hospital, in a convent nursing home and at the family apartment.

Their home consisted of an elegant fourteen-room flat and included waiting, consultation and examination rooms. The rest contained living rooms, a library, billiard room and bedrooms. It was furnished throughout with thick carpets, wood panelling, antique furniture and paintings by contemporary artists.

Kitty told me how she and Inge used to hide behind the thick velvet curtains and gawp at the beautifully dressed people emerging from carriages and chauffeur-driven cars.

They could boast to their school friends that they had real, live princesses coming to their home. These were Princess Cecilie from Prussia and her sister, Princess Alexandrine, who had Down's Syndrome. They were accompanied by a large entourage, including their security detail. Oscar treated both girls, operating on their squints. He was very fond of them both and kept cuttings of their progress as they grew up.

Other patients included sports stars like the boxer Max Schmeling, who was World Heavyweight Champion between 1930 and 1932, film directors and producers.

PRINCESSES ALEXANDRINE AND CECILIE WITH THEIR
MOTHER DUCHESS CECILIE OF MECKLENBURG-SCHWERIN

MAX SCHMELING

While the girls tried to be cool, it was sometimes hard to contain their excitement. Just days after Inge had seen a movie starring the German film star Heinz Rühmann, the real-life heart-throb turned up on their doorstep to see her father.

Hans Albers, the biggest male movie star in Germany for thirty years, was a patient. Indeed, the roll call of actors and actresses turning up at their house was like a Who's Who of German films. This can be explained by the fact that they suffered disproportionately from an eye condition caused by the widespread use of arc lights, commonly used in studios until the mid 1930s.

These ultraviolet lights were so strong, they enabled directors to shoot daytime scenes at night. The reaction to these lights, known as 'Klieg eyes' (after the lights' founder), caused actors to have red, swollen and watering eyes. Not only was it extremely uncomfortable but they simply couldn't afford the downtime. This is one of the reasons why so many actors of the period appeared in public wearing sunglasses.

Other patients included the painter Käthe Kollwitz, the composer Moritz Moszkowski, the writer Martin Beradt and the world chess champion Emanuel Lasker.

Oscar had many overseas patients. From India came the Maharaja and the Maharani of Baroda. Otto Braun, the leader of Prussia until 1932, was a patient. When, like everyone else he was requested to fill out his occupation, he duly wrote 'Prime Minister'.

HEINZ RÜHMANN

OSCAR'S SIXTIETH BIRTHDAY WAS CELEBRATED IN MANY NEWSPAPERS

In 1931, Oscar's sixtieth birthday was widely celebrated and featured in a dozen local and national newspapers. The Friday 9 October edition of the Berlin daily newspaper *Tempo* carried his photo next to its masthead on the front page.

The following year marked his twenty-fifth anniversary as chief physician in the eye department of the Rudolf Virchow Hospital. The mayor of Berlin sent his personal congratulations: 'I extend my warmest congratulations to you on this anniversary and acknowledge your loyal cooperation and the outstanding services you have rendered... May you be granted the opportunity to continue to dedicate your hard work and your wealth of knowledge to the well-being of our sick for a long time.'

On a personal level, it is clear from his patients' letters that Oscar was adored. He wrote to and received long letters from his patients concerning not only their medical issues but also their families.

His close friend Rabbi Dr G. Salzberger, wrote of Oscar: 'Members of the Imperial family, well-known artists and statesmen and even anti-Semites in high positions sought his help and support. He made no distinction between high and low. He was not concerned with material gain but even treated many patients free of charge. He took a personal interest in everyone and each one of them was blessed by his talents which extended well beyond office hours.'

Kitty observed many years later in a eulogy for her father: 'A patient was never a case but always a person in whom he took much interest, not making the slightest difference between a paying and a non-paying patient; of the latter, there were many.'

It was partly thanks to the gratitude and generosity of past patients that the family was to survive the darker years.

The girls' mother was Jeanne Traub, Oscar's second wife. His first wife, a society beauty called Toni Brieger, had been institutionalised in a mental home following the birth of their only child, Robert (Bob), in 1911. It is unknown whether this was a chronic mental health disorder or simply the result of untreated post-natal depression. The couple divorced in 1920 with Oscar marrying Jeanne the following year. She was nineteen years his junior.

DARING TO BE

INGE AND KITTY'S MOTHER, JEANNE TRAUB

JEANNE WITH KITTY, LEFT, AND INGE, RIGHT

Throughout his second marriage, Oscar continued to pay for a nurse for Toni. He kept in regular contact with the hospital and met her nursing fees. When he fled Berlin in 1939, he had instructed that his pension should be transferred to her for her care - a sum of approximately 490RM a month (then about £40) plus 11RM for her clothes. He would become distraught many years later when the Nazis cancelled his pension, leaving Toni without the funding for care. Under the Nazis, asylum patients were often deprived of food, neglected and administered lethal doses of medication. Toni would later become one of the 300,000 mentally ill and disabled people to be murdered.

Oscar's young son Bob was not allowed to see his mother and did not get on with his step-mother. After his father's marriage to Jeanne, he moved in with his grandparents but would join the family at weekends and holidays. He had his own room in the flat and the girls would be thrilled whenever he arrived.

Jeanne was a devoted wife. Kitty noted many years later in her eulogy for Oscar: 'My mother idolised my father. As his work kept him so very busy, she often accompanied him by car to his hospital or nursing home and waited there for hours until he had finished so as to spend time with him while driving.'

BOB

THE GIRLS WITH OSCAR AND BOB

As Frau Professor Fehr, it was her role to oversee the smooth running of her husband's home practice and, as was custom for an upper-middle-class family, she had a large live-in household to manage. This included the nanny, Valeska Konig, known as Dedda, who had arrived when Inge was just seven weeks old, as well as a cook, maid and chauffeur.

During the early 1920s, Germany suffered from a period of hyperinflation with prices doubling every three days in 1923. Wages paid in the morning would be virtually worthless by lunchtime.[1] Jeanne asked the housekeeper to leave first thing in the morning to buy food before prices increased during the day. She spent her time stamp-collecting, in part as a buffer against rising

ALWAYS DRESSED THE SAME. INGE, TOP LEFT, AND KITTY, RIGHT END SECOND ROW, DRESSED AS NATIVE AMERICANS

prices, and sewing identical dresses for the girls (which they wore under sufferance). The practical day-to-day childcare was delegated to Dedda.

IN THEIR SWIMSUITS AND PLAY CLOTHES

IN MATCHING RAINCOATS

PROFESSOR OSCAR FEHR

Oscar was born in Brunswick, northern Germany, in October 1871, the third child of Salomon and Helene. His father was a successful horse breeder, and the family lived in a stately old house near the town's square.

After matriculating, Oscar studied at Heidelberg, Kiel and Berlin universities, graduating in medicine summa cum laude (with the highest honours). He wished to study under the well-known ophthalmologist, Julius Hirschberg, and was accepted due to his excellent draughtman's skills. Within a few years, Oscar became the second and then first assistant, when he helped with more difficult operations.

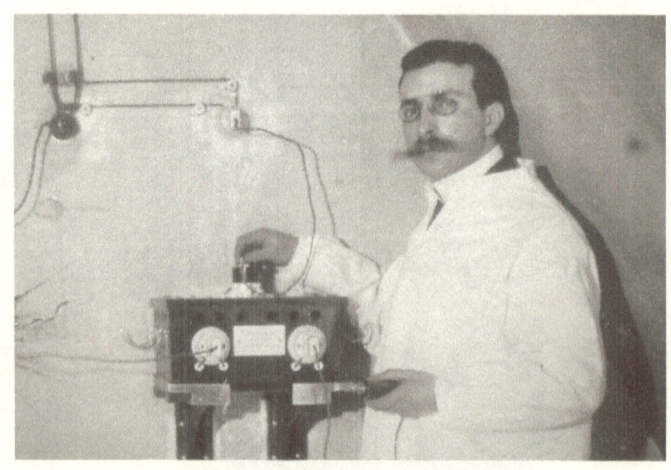

OSCAR EARLY IN HIS CAREER

OSCAR WAS KNOWN THROUGHOUT HIS LIFE FOR HIS
IMMACULATE AND DAPPER APPEARANCE

In 1906, Oscar was appointed head of the eye department of a new hospital, the Rudolf Virchow, where he remained for nearly thirty years. Initially there were only 25 beds, which grew to 120. Two to three days a week were operating days with up to ten operations performed daily. At 2 p.m. he left the clinic to attend to his private practice, where he would often work until 9 or 10 p.m.

On Saturdays, after work was finished, he took his students to a morgue where operations were carried out on cadavers. None of his staff were permitted to operate on patients until they had proven themselves in this way.

During World War 1, the Rudolf Virchow Hospital was used in part to tend to servicemen. Oscar treated the eyes of hundreds of soldiers and was subsequently awarded several military distinctions.

In total, Oscar published forty-six papers, with his research on swimming pool conjunctivitis making him known in medical circles around the world.

Under Oscar's leadership, the Rudolf Virchow Hospital's ophthalmological department became one of the most important in Germany. His staff described him as being calm, friendly and very kind.

Oscar's hobbies included painting, chess, bridge, car mechanics, walking and ice-skating.

Oscar and Jeanne threw themselves into the Berlin social scene during a period known as 'the Golden Twenties' from 1924-29 when the economy improved. After the Greater Berlin Act 1920, which expanded the size of the city, Berlin became the third-largest municipality in the world and was known as a dynamic centre for the best minds in the sciences, humanities, art, music and education. This was the era of cabaret, the Charleston, silent movies and Marlene Dietrich. Brecht unveiled *The Threepenny Opera*, Carl Jung developed new theories on psychology, and Albert Einstein won the Nobel prize for physics. Berlin also became a magnet for English writers such as W. H. Auden, Stephen Spender and Christopher Isherwood. Oscar and Jeanne were part of this circle and

OSCAR AND JEANNE FEATURED IN A CELEBRITY NEWSPAPER IN 1930

always in great demand. They mingled with the great, good and the wealthy and featured in society magazines.

Kitty reflected many years later: 'They were invited to many interesting dinner parties and balls, where they met many famous people. At Betty Stern's parties they met many actors and actresses. On one occasion when Professor Albert Einstein was my mother's partner at dinner, she disputed his theory of relativity. My mother was no mathematician!'

The family flat was situated in Keithstrasse, Berlin W62, a fashionable area of central Berlin. This was convenient for Oscar and Jeanne but also great for the girls since it was close to the Tiergarten, a large park with a zoo. The girls met their friends here and walked their beloved dachshunds, a father and son, Plisch and Plum.

Inge reminisced in a letter to Kitty on her eightieth birthday: 'You were always athletic. We were nearly every day at the zoo gymnastic area and exercised on their single and double bars. When we were smaller, we went to the sandpit and paddling pool. I remember you cried when you were told you couldn't take the hole you had dug back home with you.'

The journey to school couldn't have been easier. The school backed on to their yard and the girls could climb over their own wall. Kitty often blamed this proximity for her regular lateness.

KEITHSTRASSE, BERLIN

WITH PLISCH AND PLUM

KITTY SPENT HOURS PRACTISING GYMNASTICS

PLAYING IN THE PARK

GARDEN WALL
ONTO THE SCHOOL

KITTY, SECOND RIGHT, IN THE SCHOOL YARD BORDERING THEIR HOME

Both girls loved their school and had a wide social circle. Inge had a great memory and excelled at history, while Kitty preferred maths and the sciences. The girls were incredibly close. At Easter, when they hunted for eggs, they always ended up sharing their loot equally. In photographs from that time, Inge would frequently have placed her arm around her sister protectively. If one of them was ill, the other would create a comic book to cheer up their sibling. The main characters were Dedda and their dogs.

Despite the fact that the girls saw little of their father during the week, they had a very close bond and adored him. The highlight of the week was Sunday. Their chauffeur, Brode, would drive the family in a large sedan car into the Grunewald Forest where they would trek for hours. From there they developed a lifelong long love of walks and the countryside.

In 1935, Oscar purchased a dark-blue Horch cabriolet sedan for the substantial sum of 10,300RM (then £824). By now he was a confident driver and liked to drive the family himself. During holidays they toured the Alps, often meeting up with Bob, who was studying in Switzerland.

Although Oscar swotted up on car mechanics, there were several hair-raising moments as Kitty recalled: 'On one occasion we were driving up the Great St Bernard Pass in Switzerland when the engine of our car broke down. It was getting dark. My mother was terrified. My father skilfully let the car roll down backwards down the narrow mountain road with its many hairpin bends to the nearest village, which was a fair way off. Our nanny, Dedda, led the way with a torch. After that event we had a spotlight fitted to the car.'

On another occasion the family went skiing in Oberbaerenburg in Saxony when the Horch became stuck in snow. Kitty noted: 'Another car came to our help and got stuck itself. In the end horses had to pull out both of our cars. The driver of the helping car then introduced himself as Dr [Joseph] Goebbels' chauffeur.' This act of kindness would not have been possible a few years later when the family would have been readily identifiable as Jewish through their number plate.

The car journeys were always lively and full of conversation with Oscar at the centre. He entertained the family on these trips by reciting poetry and German literature. Goethe's *Faust* was a favourite and he could recite the first hundred pages by heart.

In contrast, the girls' relationship with their mother was not close. While Jeanne adored her husband, the same warmth and affection was not felt by the girls. As I grew up, my mother would talk warmly and frequently about her father and how kind and clever he was. About her mother, she never spoke.

ENGINE TROUBLE!

OSCAR IN THE HORCH

ON A WALKING HOLIDAY IN THE ALPS

Jeanne expected her daughters to act like young ladies: to dress smartly, be cultured and behave with decorum. She may have had some success with Inge, who enjoyed shopping and took pride in her appearance, but Kitty was a tomboy who did not live up to all her mother's ideals. Jeanne praised Inge's looks but seemed to despair of Kitty's mop of unruly hair.

While Jeanne did regularly take the girls on educational trips to museums, this was not as much fun as the Sunday walks with their father. A love of museums never materialised in later life!

If their mother could be distant and formal, Dedda provided the fun and laughter. She did not have children of her own and lavished love on the girls. By day, she wore a starched formal uniform with a cap pinned to her hair, but she wore informal clothes during the evenings, weekends and holidays. She was warm, kind and always approachable. The girls adored her.

My mother never complained of a lack of maternal warmth - she had Dedda. Their separation a decade later would be the hardest blow of all.

DEDDA

INGE AND DEDDA

HELEN JOHN

TOP: ACTUALLY HE WAS MEANT TO BE TOLD OFF
MIDDLE: IN THE HOTEL DEDDA BRINGS THE FOOD
BOTTOM: OUR PLISCH AS USUAL TURNS THE FIRST OF THREE CIRCLES

CHAPTER 2

THE RISE OF HITLER

Inge and Kitty's early childhood in the 1920s coincided with a difficult economic period for Germany.

The impact of the stock market crash in the US in October 1929 led to a period of depression. The country's Weimar Republic, set up after the end of WW1, had weathered the period of high inflation by borrowing millions of dollars from the US. The Americans, despite President Herbert Hoover's one-year moratorium in 1931, demanded urgent repayment. Across Germany and much of Europe, this resulted in a banking crisis and a surge in unemployment. The climate of fear and financial desperation played perfectly into the hands of the right-wing, anti-Semitic and anti-communist National Socialist German Workers' Party, whose member were known as Nazis.

Their leader, Adolf Hitler, blamed the Jews and communists for Germany's woes. By 1932, the Nazis were the largest political party in the German parliament, the Reichstag. In January 1933, with no other leader able to command enough support to rule, the President of Germany, Paul von Hindenburg, appointed Adolf Hitler Chancellor of Germany.

With the benefit of hindsight, the rise of Nazism should have been terrifying to behold. In truth, however, Inge and Kitty found it exciting and cool - in the beginning.

As Kitty explained to her grandson seventy years later: 'I was ten years old when the Nazis came to power. The first I heard of this was on our way home from skating on the lake near us when a boy stopped us to say he was celebrating because Hitler had come to power. Our parents didn't tell us much about politics, it was safer like this. This was quite an exciting time for young people. Girls joined the BDM (Bund Deutscher Mädel) and the boys the HJ (Hitler-Jugend). They went camping, marching and hiking and were indoctrinated with Nazi propaganda.'

In February 1933, a fire broke out in the Reichstag in Berlin and a Dutch communist confessed to starting it. This episode was used by Hitler to convince President Hindenburg to declare an emergency decree suspending many civil liberties enjoyed by German citizens, including the freedom of expression, freedom of the press and freedom to hold public assemblies, with police authorised to detain citizens without cause.

Anti-Semitic messages were everywhere and even permeated into the playground. The only known Jewish girl in Inge's class, Florrie Engel, became ostracised. When she entered the playground, the girls went to the opposite corner. Inge, who had no idea of her own Jewish heritage, was no exception. Reflecting on this time in her diary, she was ashamed that she had joined in with her classmates and had also treated Florrie badly.

Inge and Kitty were impressed by the vast processions. When their parents were away, Dedda took the girls to see a night-time march to the Chancellery, the office of the German Chancellor in Berlin, with thousands of Nazi storm troopers carrying flaming torches in the dark.

On 1 May 1933, all pupils from their school lined the route to see Hindenburg, Hitler and other Nazi leaders on their way to the Lustgarten, a park in central Berlin where Hitler and Goebbels addressed the masses.

Of this historic event, Inge observed: 'I was very embarrassed as my mother would not allow me to carry a Swastika flag as nearly all the other children did, instead I had to wave the German flag.

'I was at the kerb of a narrow street where the procession of cars passed. Hitler sat in the first open car, upright and motionless.

'I don't remember much about the speeches. Hitler made a lot of noise.'

HUGE CROWDS TURNED OUT TO WATCH THE NAZI PROCESSIONS AT THE FIRST OF MAY PARADE 1933, WATCHED BY INGE AND KITTY

Some of their parents' reticence must have been picked up by ten-year-old Kitty, who had not been swept up by her classmates' enthusiasm for Nazism. At school the children had to rise before and after each lesson, raise their right hand and say 'Heil Hitler'. But Kitty was reluctant. For a while she avoided detection by standing behind a taller pupil, but one day she was spotted. She had to stand in front of the class for half an hour and 'Heil Hitler' all by herself. This must have been hard for Kitty, who was not an attention-seeker and was rarely naughty.

KITTY AT SCHOOL

KITTY'S CLASS'S HEIL HITLER ON A SCHOOL TRIP IN FRONT OF THE NAZI FLAG

The school curriculum was rapidly becoming 'Nazified'. In music classes the girls sang exclusively Nazi songs which included the 'Horst Wessel Song' (the official anthem of the Nazi Party) and 'Es zittern die morschen Knochen' (The Brittle Bones are Trembling), which includes the verse 'Today Germany belongs to us, tomorrow the whole world' – a chilling indication of the extent of Hitler's ambitions even in the mid-1930s.

Meanwhile, a new subject appeared on the curriculum, given maximum prominence and was taught daily. It was known as 'Race Knowledge'.

Inge wrote: 'We learnt about the superiority of the German race. We were told that Germans and Scandinavians had descended from the blue-eyed geese, while the rest of mankind had descended from monkeys. Jews were descended from Negroes.

'Miss Dummer, my form tutor, who was my father's patient, took me aside after the first lesson and said to me "Please ignore the rubbish I am forced to teach you."'

The girls had grown up proud in the knowledge that their second cousin, Käte Kleefeld, a society beauty, had married the former German Chancellor Gustav Stresemann. Both of Käte's parents had been born Jewish but raised their children as Lutheran. Inge was shocked to learn that this was now a source of shame.

'When the headmaster said in history one day, "Today we are going to learn about Gustav Stresemann",

I was just about to put my hand up to say that he was my uncle, when Herr Waldeck continued, "The only bad thing that can be said about Stresemann is that he has a Jewish wife." I was glad I had kept my mouth shut.'

During the course of 1933, Hitler consolidated his position with his power growing at an extraordinary rate. In July all other political parties were banned, with Germany becoming a single-party state. This included not only the communists, whose politicians were arrested and sent to concentration camps, but also the influential Social Democratic Party (SPD). Across Germany, 3,000 SPD politicians and officials were arrested, tortured and imprisoned. The other parties were intimidated into

BURNING JEWISH BOOKS, BERLIN, MAY 1933

disbanding themselves rather than face the fate of the communists and SPD. Cultural and scientific 'cleansings' took place with everything deemed 'un-German' disappearing. This included the burning of books by Jewish and left-wing writers.

On one November afternoon in 1933 everything would change suddenly for Inge and Kitty - it marked the end of their carefree childhood.

Inge, at nearly twelve, was desperate to join the Deutsche Mädel like her friends but had been forbidden by their mother, who distrusted Hitler.

'All my friends joined the Hitler Youth and were telling me about the wonderful times they were having with outings, camping, meetings and marches wearing their smart uniforms of black skirt, white blouse, black triangular scarf and brown Kletterweste (military jackets).'

Feeling miffed that she couldn't join in, Inge volunteered to collect money for the 'Winter Relief Fund', a charity that purportedly helped the poor but in reality raised money for the Nazi Party. The girls went to the large school hall waiting to be paired with a member of the Hitler Youth.

'When it came to my turn the Hitler Youth leader said, "Inge Fehr, you know very well why you can't collect." I was surprised and said that I had no idea. She answered, "Your father is a Jew." I was stunned and said that this was impossible. I had been taught that a Jew was the lowest form of life, my wonderful father could not be a Jew.

'When I came back from school I said to my father, "Papa, how could they say you are a Jew?" He replied, "It is true."

'I was shattered, I thought it was my punishment for having treated Florrie like the rest of the class did. Now we made friends, but she soon left Germany with her family.'

Although both girls and their mother were practising Lutherans, the Nazis decreed that anyone with three or four Jewish grandparents was Jewish. With two Jewish grandparents on Oscar's side and one on their mother's, the girls were classified as fully Jewish. This was not a race nor a religion with which they had ever identified, which made the upcoming persecution even more mystifying to them. They too were becoming indoctrinated with the anti-Jewish propaganda.

Inge wrote angrily in her diary: 'Just because Hitler says I'm Jewish, I'm not Jewish. I'll never be Jewish.'

Over the coming months and years some long-standing friends were forbidden to play with the girls. Inge's best friend, Marli Mussett, was the daughter of a high-ranking Nazi officer who stopped his daughter from inviting Inge to their house. However, unbeknown

KITTY MAINTAINED SEVERAL CLOSE FRIENDSHIPS DESPITE THE RAMPANT ANTI-SEMITISM THROUGHOUT BERLIN. RIGHT: ON THE SWING WITH HER BEST FRIEND, ROSERIE

to Herr Mussett, the girls remained friends in school. Some others would not sit next to Inge because 'Jewish blood stinks.'

Kitty was a little luckier than Inge, since her best friends Brigitte, Rosalie and Gisela were mischling (mixed blood) with two Jewish grandparents. This was also referred to as being non-Aryan or part-Jew. The girls continued their friendships throughout the 1930s and as the world outside became more hostile, their closeness only intensified.

Not only were Jews ostracised in society, it was becoming increasingly impossible for them to lead a professional life. The career Oscar had built up over three decades was about to come crashing down.

On 24 January 1934, just two years after the mayor of Berlin had personally expressed his wish that Oscar would work for many more years, the mayor's office wrote to Oscar forbidding him, as a Jew, from entering the Rudolf Virchow Hospital from where he had worked for a quarter of a century. For now, he was still able to work from the family home and a convent nursing home.

In August 1934, President Hindenburg died, with Hitler proclaiming himself Führer of Germany. To him, this meant more than the literal translation of 'leader' - he was to be an unassailable political force.

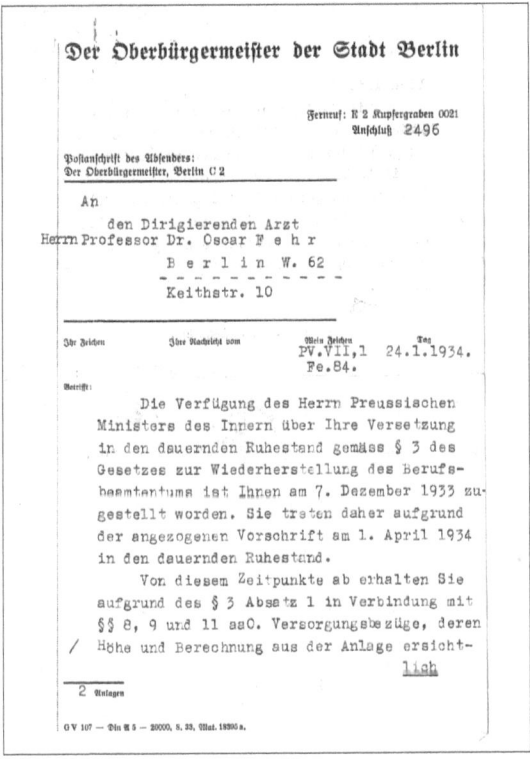

OSCAR WAS NOTIFIED HE WAS TO STOP WORKING AT THE HOSPITAL UNDER THE LAW FOR THE RESTORATION OF THE PROFESSIONAL CIVIL SERVICE

The anti-Semitic laws grew apace, ending the livelihoods of the country's half-a-million Jews. Over the coming years more than 400 decrees and regulations were passed restricting the professional and personal lives of Jews, now formally defined under the Nuremburg Laws. Jews were banned from the civil service and tax inspectors' licences were revoked. Jews were banned from performing on stage, from working as lawyers and notaries, while health insurance funds would no longer reimburse Jewish doctors. Jews were required to register all their property and assets, and Jewish workers and managers were increasingly dismissed from their jobs. Gradually, Jewish-owned companies were sold at well below market rate to non-Jewish Germans.

James Grover Macdonald, the League of Nations High Commissioner for Refugees, resigned in protest about the way that Jews were being treated, stating: 'Relentlessly the Jews and the non-Aryans are excluded from all public office and any part of the cultural and intellectual life in Germany. They are subjected to every type of humiliation. It is becoming increasingly difficult for Jews and non-Aryans to sustain life.'[2]

In March 1936, Inge and Kitty came back from school to find their mother and Dedda in tears. Yet another law had been passed, this time banning German women under forty-five from working with Jews. They thought

DARING TO BE

INGE

KITTY AND INGE IN CLASSIC DIRNDL DRESSES

Dedda would need to leave, but a later amendment stated that servants who had been working for Jews for more than ten years could stay since they were verjudet - a derogatory word by the Nazis meaning Judaized.

The Fehr family didn't conform to the Nazis' stereotype of what Jewish people should look like. In some ways Inge resembled a classic Aryan beauty with high cheekbones and clear blue eyes. Her fine features, together with her traditional dirndl dress, caught the attention of two Nazi storm troopers, known as the *Sturmabteilung*, who asked Inge and her friend to pose with a collecting tin.

'They looked at us all and finally picked out myself and another girl. One gave me money to put in the collection tin while the other SA man took photographs. Out of a class of 24 they had managed to pick out one Swiss girl, the only foreigner, and myself - the only non-Aryan.' Her classmates never mentioned to the SA photographer that Inge was considered Jewish - being passed off as an Aryan would embolden her in later years.

The photo appeared in the Nazi Party's propaganda newspaper *Völkischer Beobachter* (the People's Observer) and was captioned 'German Girls Give to the Winter Relief Fund' - the same fund Inge had been banned from collecting for in November 1933.

* * *

On 9 April 1937 the mayor of Berlin banned Jewish children from state schools, the biggest change so far for Inge and Kitty. This was followed by a decree from the Nazi Ministry for Science and Education that: 'It is unacceptable to expect that any German teacher provide instruction to Jewish schoolchildren. It should be self-evident that it is intolerable for German schoolchildren to sit in a classroom shared with Jews.'[3]

Jeanne was not going to allow her daughters to suffer the humiliation of being turned away from school. Days before the decree was due to be enacted, Jeanne moved them to the Jewish Goldschmidt Schule, a fee-paying school set up two years before by historian and English specialist Dr Leonore Goldschmidt.

It was heart-breaking for the girls, who were separated from those classmates they still considered friends mid-term and felt they were being sent to a ghetto. Despite rabid anti-Semitism, they still enjoyed school.

Having been subjected to the Nazi indoctrination, Inge's first impressions of the Goldschmidt school were not favourable: 'The first time in the new class. We have a teacher as old as Methuselah and as round as a billiard ball. I don't like it at all in this school. Way too Jewish.'

Over time, however, the girls were pleasantly surprised. Although Hitler Youth boys shouted abuse at the children coming in, the school represented a sanctuary. Tight bonds and close friendships were formed between pupils, some of whom had been left friendless at their former schools.

GOLDSCHMIDT SCHULE

By the time Inge and Kitty arrived, there were 500 boys and girls, taught by forty teachers. Dr Goldschmidt had the foresight to prioritise English and used the British curriculum, to prepare the children for any future emigration to the UK and America. One teacher even specialised in Saxon history using the textbook *Our Island Story* - Inge and Kitty learnt about Ethelred the Unready and King Alfred's burning of the cakes. Another teacher insisted his pupils learn Mark Antony's entire speech from *Julius Caesar*, complete with the correct English pronunciation and grammar.[4]

Inge and Kitty were taken aback by the high standards demanded and the cleverness of the other pupils. Inge wrote: 'Having learnt at school how awful the Jews were (I thought we were the exception), I was very surprised to find how nice the other pupils were, how brilliant at lessons and how good at sports.'

Inge and Kitty had always been marked good or very good in lessons at their previous school. At Goldschmidt Schule, however, most of their subjects were graded as satisfactory or even inadequate. Inge even had to repeat a year since her grades were not good enough.

With thousands of Jewish teachers sacked from their schools, Dr Goldschmidt had been able to recruit the very best. Former pupils later praised the excellence of the teaching, the dedication of staff and the instilling of dignity and self-respect in children who had previously seen themselves as outcasts. In fact, the Goldschmidt Schule was geared at an educational elite and provided a far superior education to German state schools. One school inspector commentated: 'You have more time to teach culture because the regulations on teaching Nazi doctrine don't apply to your school.'

Female pupils swam, played tennis and trained in athletics. Since 1933, Jewish athletes had been expelled from organised athletics and banned from national teams. Even the few Jews who competed in the notorious 1936 Berlin Olympics had faced discrimination. Jews therefore had to run their own competitions and the Berlin Jewish Communal Organisation constructed the Jewish Sports stadium (Judische Sportsstadion) in the Grunwald district of Berlin, near the school. An annual highlight was the Germany-wide Jewish Sports Festival, where pupils competed in boxing, wrestling, fencing, tennis and track and field. To the girls' delight, the Goldschmidt Schule came second. A special song was composed for the games that began with the words 'Jewish youth, be strong and firm'. Dr Goldschmidt's daughter, Gertrud, who was one of the school's thirty-five competitors, wrote many years later: 'The importance of the yearly Jewish sports festival cannot be underestimated, as it established great pride in the

KITTY'S SCHOOL REPORT – MARKED GOOD IN RELIGION, LATIN
AND PHYSICAL EDUCATION. ALL OTHER SUBJECTS WERE
DEEMED SATISFACTORY OR INADEQUATE

KITTY AT THE GYM: SHE WAS DELIGHTED BY THE
PRESENCE OF SPORT ON THE CURRICULUM

TRACK AND FIELD COMPETITION, GERTRUD GOLDSCHMIDT, DAUGHTER OF THE FOUNDER LEONORE GOLDSCHMIDT, IS CENTRE REACHING BACK FOR THE BATON

athletic ability of the Jewish children and acted as counter-propaganda to constant Jewish vilification.'[5] However, as the medal ceremony began on a balmy September afternoon in 1937, the smell of gunpower wafted over the closing proceedings. The German Army Units had set up anti-aircraft guns outside the grounds, which cast a shadow over the hitherto upbeat festivities. Everything for the Jewish community was about to become far, far worse.

DR LEONORE GOLDSCHMIDT

Dr Leonore Goldschmidt (born Tacke) was a historian, English specialist and headmistress. She anticipated the horrors likely to face her students and with extraordinary foresight, remained one step ahead of Hitler. 'Education,' she said, 'is our highest good and sometimes it can even serve as a survival tool.'

Since she was married to a Jew, she was banned from teaching in German state schools so moved to the Privaten Jüdischen Waldschule Grunewald. In the summer of 1934, her cousin, Alexander Zweig, and his wife were murdered in a purge of political opponents, known as the Night of the Long Knives. Leonore and her husband, Ernst, received a substantial inheritance from them, which they used to open a private Jewish boarding and day school in Berlin-Grunewald, a wooded, stylish suburb. The four-storey villa was converted into classrooms, with its large grounds and orchard providing plenty of space for exercise and playtime.

Before school, boarders would go for a cycle ride and swim in the Grunewaldsee lake as the use of public pools was forbidden to Jewish children. School started at 8.15 a.m. and continued until about 2 p.m. when most children went home. Pupils had the option of staying for lunch and afternoon sports. These included Danish long ball, which was a cross between rounders and baseball, handball or football. There was also a well-equipped gym. Leonore employed Jewish teachers, who were specialists in their subjects, such as science, languages and history. Former pupils reported that they were strict, demanding but fair.

At the end of May 1937, according to the national school census (Fragebogen für höhere Schulen), there were 76 pupils enrolled in the primary school and 423 pupils in the upper school. Eleven pupils were listed as Protestant, 1 was Catholic, 7 had no religious affiliation, 3 were listed as part-Jewish, 440 as Jewish and 37 had no religion stated. Fifty-six pupils in the school were listed as stateless.

Annual fees ranged from 360RM (then £28.80) to 770RM (then £61.60) but those parents unable to pay this were asked to pay what they could afford.

The ethos of the school was to educate the children bilingually and thereby prepare them for inevitable emigration to English-speaking countries. Leonore reached out to her former professor, Walter Hübner, now the chief inspector for schools, and persuaded him to allow her school to become a recognised exam centre for the University of Cambridge in 1936. After much internal debate within the department, permission was granted, and Goldschmidt Schule pupils became the first in Berlin to be prepared for entrance to UK universities.

With the increasing number of assaults on Jews, Leonore was aware that the school was fighting for survival. With extraordinary foresight, she sold it to her young English teacher, Philip Woolley, for 10RM (then about 80p).

In November 1938, when SS soldiers arrived with petrol, announcing that the school was to be burnt down, Leonore retrieved the article of sale, proving it was owned by a foreigner and claiming the destruction of property would lead to an international incident. Somewhat confused, the soldiers left, allowing Leonore a temporary reprieve.

Six months later the school was moved to a smaller villa and in July 1939, the Goldschmidt family emigrated to England. Within a couple of months they had obtained a boarding school in Folkestone for youngsters who had emigrated to England on the Kindertransport, the organised passage of unaccompanied Jewish children in the Reich to the UK between 1938-39. As more refugees gravitated to the school, it expanded across the road. Since the children had virtually no contact with their families in Germany, the school provided a home from home, celebrating children's birthdays and encouraging reading and singing in German.

In May 1940, Ernst was interned and Leonore and her students were evacuated to South Wales. After the war, she continued her teaching career in England. Leonore died in London in 1983, aged eighty-five.[6]

A photo of Oscar performing an eye operation using cocaine as an anaesthetic appeared in the illustrated weekly newspaper *Die Woche* (The Week). The following day, an article appeared in the SS newspaper *Das Schwarze Korps* (The Black Corps) with the headline 'This is still possible today. The long cast-off Jew Fehr, who has sucked so

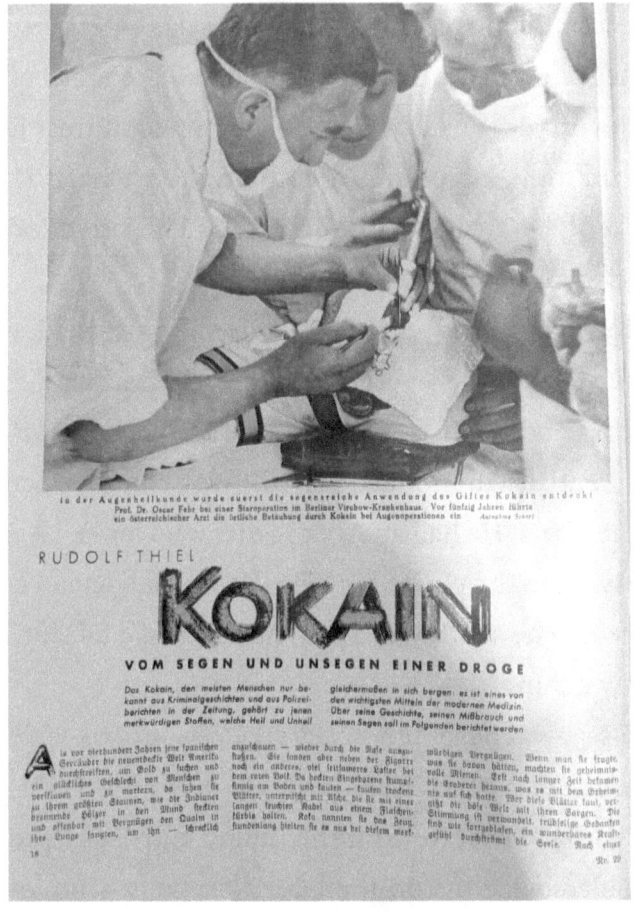

OSCAR IN *DIE WOCHE* ON 17 JULY 1935

much blood out of the German people.' Ironically, Oscar had been well-known for his very reasonable fees, waiving them for those who couldn't pay.

On 10 August 1938 a letter arrived informing Oscar that he was no longer allowed to practice but he could apply to the Minister of the Interior for permission to treat Jews. With his application supported by the Crown Princess Cecilie of Prussia, whose daughters he had treated a few years earlier, Oscar joined the ranks of the 175 Jewish doctors and dentists permitted to treat Jews. He had to fix a blue shield with a yellow Star of David marked 'Jew-Treater' at the door and all his prescriptions were stamped with a Jewish star.

By now Jews were being openly attacked with impunity. These included some of Oscar's fellow doctors and dentists. Inge witnessed one such attack: 'My dentist, who looked Jewish, was being beaten up by the Nazis. He had an Aryan wife, who looked Aryan. She went to the police for help. So the policeman came and when he saw it was a Jew, he just stood by laughing and watching.'

Oscar was never physically attacked but was excluded from the life he had enjoyed. He was an outcast and forced to withdraw from his many clubs and professional associations on the basis that he was no longer considered to be a citizen of the Reich according to the

Reich citizenship Law of 15 September 1935. This stated: 'A Jew cannot be a citizen of the Reich. He cannot exercise the right to vote; he cannot hold public office.'[7]

Having been a respected member of the German establishment, Oscar and his family were rapidly becoming persona non grata. Emotions ranged from anger and hurt to misplaced optimism that the tide would turn with normality restored.

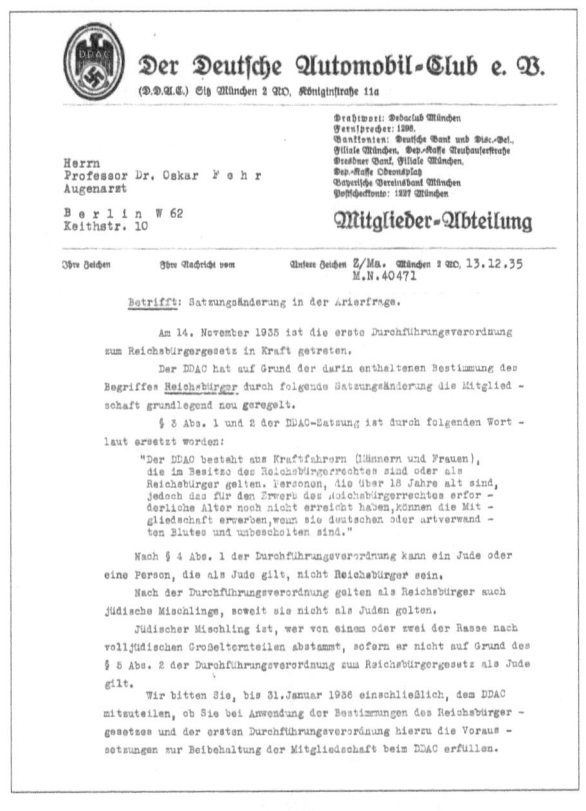

LETTER BANNING OSCAR FROM MEMBERSHIP OF
THE GERMAN AUTOMOBILE CLUB

On 15 September 1938, all cars belonging to Jews had to get a distinctive Jewish number plate, a number over 300,000. Without doubt, the Fehr family car would have been smashed up or pelted with stones and so, with a heavy heart, the Horch was sold. This presented an obstacle to Oscar, as although his car was a passion it was also integral to his work. By December of that year, there was a blanket ban on Jews driving.

While many erstwhile friends abandoned the family, some remained loyal. An Aryan former patient, Mrs Emmy Lignitz, came to the rescue despite the personal risks to her and her family. If caught, she could have faced imprisonment, or worse.

Oscar always remembered this kindness and bravery, commenting many years later: 'When I was not allowed any more to use my car, Mrs Lignitz drove me with her own car on all my professional ways [journeys]. She did so almost daily, until our emigration, disregarding the great danger to which she exposed herself.'

Throughout Germany, even churches were becoming Nazified.

Under Hitler, the Protestant church had split into two, the Confessing Church and German Christians, who set about purging their churches of what they considered to be Jewish influence, dismissing the Old Testament, based on the Hebrew Bible, and banning non-Aryans from serving in the church. They called themselves 'Storm troopers for Christ'. In line with Nazi philosophy, church leaders and members of their congregation would be defined not by their religion but by their race. Church services became ever larger and more spectacular, with Nazi flags on the altar, Nazi songs sung by the congregation and Nazi greetings at the door. They were led locally by a minister called Pastor Hauk, who told his congregations that Christ was not a Jew - that was a biblical error - but an immigrant in Palestine of impeccable Aryan descent. The Fehrs were members of the anti-Nazi Confessing Church locally led by Pastor Gerhard Jacobi at the Friedrich Wilhelm Memorial Church. The two pastors launched into an unbecoming physical fight in a church after Pastor Jacobi tried to prevent Pastor

PASTOR GERHARD JACOBI

Hauk from placing a picture of Hitler on the altar. Jacobi was punched so hard that his glasses cracked. Oscar fitted him with a new pair after an emergency visit to his home practice.

In the new world of persecution, the girls found a safe space in Jacobi's church, where Aryans and non-Aryans were welcomed equally. Here they were seen as Christians, which is how they saw themselves. It helped restore their self-confidence and some sense of normality. However, the church teachings fell on deaf ears at home, since Jeanne hated the Nazis and certainly didn't want to forgive them for their sins. She had little patience with what she saw as Kitty's burgeoning religious zealotry. Kitty moaned in her diary: 'Mutti says she'll never be a good Christian because she wants to hate her enemies. What am I expected to say to that?'

The girls adored Pastor Jacobi and Kitty spent her spare time in Bible class as she prepared for her confirmation. The pastor's sermons seemed to have great relevance to the tribulations the family were facing - that however bad things were, these wouldn't separate her from God's love. Kitty wrote: 'Father Jacobi read a passage from the Bible, Romans 8, beginning with "If God is for us, what can be against us". Then he spoke about it quite fabulously, so personally, he couldn't have said it to everyone. It wouldn't have taken much for me to start crying.'

In May 1936 the Confession Church wrote a firm but polite memorandum to Hitler protesting at the Reich's anti-Christian tendencies, the persecution of Jews and the interference of the running of the Protestant Church.

Hitler responded by arresting hundreds of pastors, including Jacobi, and murdering their legal adviser, Dr Friedrich Weißler, in Sachsenhausen concentration camp. In addition, the church's funds were confiscated and they were forbidden from collecting donations in offertories.

Kitty lamented the occasional absences of the pastor, not knowing that he and many of his colleagues were often arrested. The *New York Times* reported on New Year's Eve: 'The secret political police rearrested Pastor Gerhard Jacobi, chairman of the Berlin-Brandenburg Confessional Synod, today and will keep him under arrest over New Year's to prevent his preaching. He was also kept under arrest in his apartment over Christmas. He was scheduled to preach at a New Year's Eve service at 11 o'clock tonight in his church.' The pastor and his ministers were released in the New Year once church attendances had declined. On another occasion the paper reported that the pastor was flanked by fifty bodyguards to enable him to reach the pulpit.

Over time Kitty noticed that 'pastors and entire congregations no longer want to belong to the confessional church and have left, they are just too tired to fight for it.'

Any sense that the growing tide of persecution could be controlled evaporated on 9 November 1938 when the girls saw a column of smoke on their way to school. Inge wrote: 'We were reading *Macbeth* when our headmistress, Frau Dr Goldschmidt, entered in tears to tell us that a pogrom was in progress. We were all to leave quickly, simply by the back door and not to return to school until further notice.

'On my way home, I followed the smoke and arrived at the synagogue in the Fasanenstrasse, which had been set alight. Crowds were watching from the opposite pavement. Then I passed through the Tauentzienstrasse, where I saw crowds smashing Jewish shop windows and jeering as the owners were trying to salvage their goods.'

This was the start of Kristallnacht, also known as the Night of Broken Glass, named after the shards of glass that littered the streets of Jewish-owned buildings while synagogues were smashed to pieces. It was started by the Nazis paramilitary forces with participation from the Hitler Youth, many wearing civilian clothes to support the perception that the disturbances were initiated by the public, while the police watched on.

This followed Goebbels' instructions, while speaking at the anniversary of the Beer Hall Putsch, that 'the

SYNAGOGUE IN FASANENSTRASSE - DESTROYED BY ARSON

police should be withdrawn. For once the Jews should get the feel of popular anger.'[8]

When Inge and Kitty arrived home, they were shocked to discover the words 'FEHR JUDE' (Fehr-Jew) scrawled in bold red paint on the pavement outside their building. This turned out to be the handiwork of their long-time former employee, Gerhard Brode, a recent recruit to the Nazi Party. Oscar had first met Brode in 1926 when he was a starving, unemployed young man and had given him a job. Brode had driven the family on their Sunday outings as well as for holidays to the mountains. Oscar, Inge and Kitty had trusted him as an extended member of their family. Jeanne, however, had never liked him.

Brode, it emerged, was bitter. After Oscar had taken to driving himself, Brode had been re-employed as a doorman/receptionist but had been sacked for embezzling money. As well as painting the pavement by their doorstep, Brode blackmailed Oscar for 1,000 marks (then £80), threatening to tell the Gestapo about the family's privately expressed views about the Nazis. Inge noted: 'My father had to pay as in the Third Reich, a Jew had no chance against a storm trooper.'

On the evening of Kristalnacht, Oscar received a phone call from a well-wisher advising him that Jewish men were about to be rounded up and sent to concentration camps. Oscar left immediately to stay with his niece

TREACHEROUS BRODE IN WHITE CHAUFFEUR'S CAP

in Dresden, checking in with Jeanne daily via a secret code on the telephone.

The full horror of Kristallnacht became clear the next day. Across the country, Jewish homes, hospitals and schools had been ransacked and attacked with sledgehammers and 30,000 Jewish men had been arrested and taken into 'protective custody' in police stations, schools and prisons. While a third of them stayed in these local custody points, the rest were transferred to either Dachau, Sachsenhausen or Buschewald concentration camps. While most were subsequently released, around 500 died in concentration camps from illnesses, overexertion and lack of medication. After their release, around 600 emergency amputations were necessitated as a result of severe frostbite and untreated wounds.

Foreign correspondent and subsequent Director-General of the BBC Hugh Carleton Greene reported for the *Daily Telegraph*: 'I have seen several anti-Jewish outbreaks in Germany during the past five years but nothing as nauseating as this. Racial hatred and hysteria seemed to have taken over otherwise decent people. I saw fashionably dressed women clapping their hands and screaming with glee while respectable middle-class mothers held up their babies to see the "fun".'[9]

For the previous two years Oscar's son Bob, who had left Berlin University to study engineering in

MASS ARREST OF JEWISH MEN IN BADEN-BADEN AFTER THE POGROM OF 9-10 NOVEMBER 1938 (SOURCE: GERMAN FEDERAL ARCHIVES)

Switzerland, had urged his family to leave the country. In common with many Jews of the time, Oscar had always believed things would get better, but no longer. Kitty later reflected that this presented a turning point for the family: 'Before the Night of the Broken Glass my father thought that the Nazis would not last and did not consider leaving Germany, there was so much to give up and he loved the culture of the country. But after that night we knew we had to leave.'

With Oscar treating Jews every day, he learnt about the harsh reality of the persecution others were facing. Since Hitler had come to power, concentration camps were being created across Germany. Unlike prisons, these were independent of any judicial review and were intended to remove those seen as a security threat - usually communists, Jews, Romani people, homosexuals and the disabled. Away from public and judicial scrutiny, they would be used to murder some individuals and groups. Although the prisoners were undernourished and mistreated, the camps were not at this point the mass extermination camps they would become after 1941. From then on, rather than focusing on isolating Jews in ghettos, or forcing them to emigrate, the Nazis created purpose-built killing centres.

In the late 1930s, however, for the tens of thousands of Jews incarcerated in Dachau, Buchenwald and Sachsenhausen concentration camps, it was still possible to leave once evidence of eligibility to emigrate had been provided. Since Oscar treated only Jewish patients, he was hearing terrible tales about those who had managed to escape. Jeanne wrote: 'The anxiety and strain of that time is unforgettable. We were deeply touched by the misery of our many friends and patients, who came straight from the concentration camps to consult with my husband.'

The Goldschmidt Schule became a source of intelligence gathering. Kitty remembered pupils being asked every day who had fathers in concentration camps. 'Many children put their hands up. They were then asked whether any of them had escaped and if so, how.'

Jeanne's sister, Alice Kielland, arrived from Norway with her husband Christian and offered to take the girls back to live with them. Christian was a famous and elderly gynaecologist who gave his name to the widely used Kielland forceps for delivery. After much consideration, it was decided that the family should stay together and the girls would remain in Berlin, for now. In retrospect, this was a fortuitous decision since Norway was to surrender to the Germans in 1940.

Another decree in November 1938 further restricted the movement of all Jews. Across the country, Jewish children could not attend German state schools. The girls could no longer go to any form of entertainment like swimming pools, cinemas, theatres, libraries, circuses, concerts or zoos. They were forbidden to sit on park benches, only on yellow benches marked 'Judenbank'. They were also banned from walking on any of the main streets. The penalties were serious. One of their friends had a relative killed by the Gestapo, the Nazi secret police, for concealing her Star of David under a raincoat.

Oscar came home after three weeks when no one had arrived to arrest him. He had been fortunate. As backup, the Lignitzs gave Oscar a key to their apartment where the Fehr family could hide if necessary. This kindness was in stark contrast to previous Aryan friends who would no longer have anything to do with them.

YELLOW BENCH FOR JEWS ONLY

SIGN STATING THAT JEWS ARE NOT WANTED HERE

Oscar wrote: 'We owe deepest gratitude to Mr and Mrs Lignitz. They made life under the Nazi terror tolerable to us and they helped us to keep [the] belief in mankind we were going to lose after the disappointment caused by so many old friends and acquaintances.'

Increasingly, fingers would be pointed at the Fehrs when they went out. Not even their dachshunds, Plisch and Plum, were immune from racist taunts. Kitty wrote: 'When Inge walked the dogs, a woman called hers back saying "don't play with these Jewish dogs". On this occasion, Inge had the satisfaction of replying that her pedigree dogs should not mix with mongrels.'

At school, the girls found that most of their male Jewish teachers had been arrested and placed in concentration camps. The female Jewish teachers remained for now.

With the unrelenting speed of Jewish persecution, it was a race against time to escape, but the Nazis had confiscated their passports. Since October 1938 the Ministry for the Interior had invalidated all German passports held by Jews until they had been reissued and stamped with the letter J. Jewish women had to add 'SARA' as their middle name and Jewish men 'ISRAEL'. Oscar had to write to his patients on notepaper stamped with a Star of David informing them his name had been changed to Oscar Israel Fehr.

INGE WITH PLISCH

OSCAR WITH PLISCH AND PLUM

Meanwhile the girls had their fingerprints and photographs taken of their left profile for their Kenncarten (Jewish identity cards), which were marked with an oversized J. The design made their subjects look like criminals.

Oscar was luckier than most since he had influential contacts. He was successful in his application for the family to move to Luxembourg, but he was not offered a work permit and therefore would be unable to support the family.

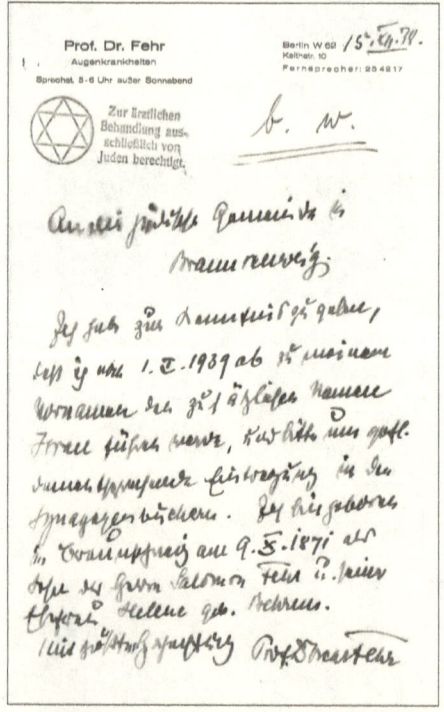

LETTER TO PATIENTS INFORMING THEM THAT OSCAR WAS TO BE KNOWN AS OSCAR ISRAEL FEHR

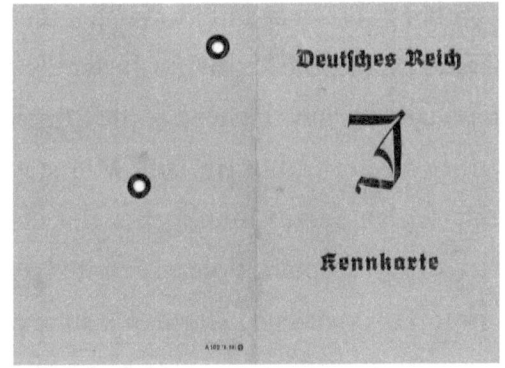

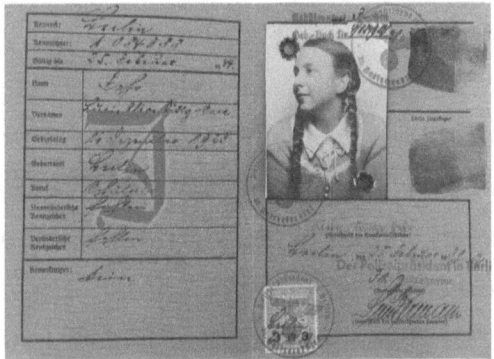

KITTY'S KENNKARTE

OSCAR'S KENNKARTE

In November 1938 Oscar and Jeanne met the man who was ultimately responsible for saving the family's lives. He was Frank Foley, officially the head of the British Passport Control Office in Berlin but, in fact, MI6 station chief running the British Secret Intelligence Service station. From 1922 to 1939, Captain Foley recruited agents and acquired important details of German military research and development. He was reported to be a brilliant agent.

Captain Foley is often referred to as the 'British Schindler' due to the estimated 10,000 Jewish people he helped save. During the mid to late 1930s he expedited visas to help Jews escape from Germany. Hundreds of desperate Jewish families thronged the streets outside Captain Foley's office in the British Embassy on a daily basis. Journalist James Holborn of the *Glasgow Herald* reported: 'Desperate Jews continue to flock to the British control offices ... in the hope of gaining admission to Great Britain, Palestine or one of the Crown Colonies ... families were often represented by womenfolk, many of them in tears, while the men of the family waited in concentration camps until some evidence of likelihood of emigration could be shown to the secret police.'

According to his wife Kay: 'He would handle as many applications himself as he could manage, and he would walk amongst his staff of examiners to see where he could assist them, or give words of comfort to those who waited.'

Defying the Foreign Office, Captain Foley bent the rules very liberally to avoid some of the impossibly difficult exit requirements. Where, for instance, £1,000 was required for a visa to Palestine, he would on occasions issue a visa for needy applicants with just £10. His help extended to advising applicants on how to secure fake passports. A young man, Wim van Leer, who had been sent by the Quakers to assist, noted: 'I learnt a lot from him. Where to get genuine fake passports, mainly from South American banana republics; the names of small, helpful printshops willing to produce one-off forms; rubber-stamp makers on whose discretion one could rely, and a number of escape routes and procedures.'[10]

Yad Vashem, the World Holocaust Remembrance Centre, cites the case of sixteen-year-old Miriam Posner who sought a visa to Palestine: 'Foley saved my life. We heard that there was this man Foley who was kind to the Jews. My mother begged him. He just paced up and down a little and then asked for my passport and put the visa stamp on it. He did not ask any questions.'

Captain Foley is known to have visited the newly built Sachsenhausen concentration camp, 40 km from Berlin, presenting visas to the authorities so they would release the named Jews from custody.

Foley had great admiration for Oscar's work and developed a personal interest in the welfare of the whole family.

CAPTAIN FRANK FOLEY

After serving in World War I, Foley was noted for his daring and his excellent language skills. Consequently, he was enlisted into a small unit in the Intelligence Corps in 1918, responsible for running networks of secret agents in France, Belgium and the Netherlands. He was subsequently recruited by MI6.

Captain Foley realised that to survive, the Jews had to escape from Nazi Germany, but they faced an often impossible bureaucratic obstacle course. His embassy was besieged by desperate families. With queues outside sometimes reaching a mile in length, he sent strongly worded cables pleading for extra blank visa certificates and staff to help. Regarding the Nazis as 'the rule of Satan upon earth' (according to Benno Cohen, Chairman of the Zionist Organisation of Germany), he worked from 7 a.m. to 10 p.m. Cohen described Foley as 'The Scarlet Pimpernel of the Jews'.

Foley was honoured posthumously in 2018 by the British Intelligence Agency, MI6, for enabling 10,000 German Jews to escape to the UK or Palestine prior to World War II. The organisation's chief, Alex Younger, said: 'Frank's dignity, compassion and bravery are in no doubt. As a consummately effective intelligence officer, he witnessed at first hand the Nazi seizure of power, and the horrors and depravity of the regime. With little regard for his personal safety, he took a stance against evil. He knew the dire consequences were he to get caught. Frank's tenacity and passion saved the lives of many thousands of European Jews.'

Following Kristallnacht, the Foleys hid Jewish families in their home, including Leo Baeck, a renowned rabbi and chairman of the Association of German Rabbis. Captain Foley was moved from Germany in 1939 but left behind visas with instructions to distribute them to those seeking to escape the Nazis.

In January 1941 he was awarded Companion of the Order of St Michael and St George for his services to the Foreign Office. Later that year he was given the task of questioning Hitler's deputy, Rudolf Hess, after Hess's flight to Scotland. After the war he returned to Berlin as Assistant Inspector General at the Control Commission for Germany,

> where he hunted for Nazi war criminals. He retired to Worcestershire in 1949 and died in 1958, aged seventy-four.
>
> One of the Jewish leaders in pre-war Berlin, Hans Friedenthal, wrote to him in 1942: 'We Jews have no order to award but we have a good and long memory. You may be assured that the German Jews will not forget how often you have helped them.'
>
> In 1999, Yad Vashem accorded him the honour of one of the 'Righteous Among the Nations'. In 2004, a plaque was unveiled at the British Embassy in Berlin and, in 2010, he was awarded the title of British Hero of the Holocaust by the British government. In 2018, MI6 unveiled a bust of Frank Foley at its London headquarters.[11]

On Christmas Day 1938 the phone rang in the Fehr household. To Oscar and Jeanne's surprise, it was Captain Foley himself with the best Christmas present imaginable: the family's application for a visa to the UK had been successful.

This was confirmed in writing a few days later with a request that the family should post their passports and would receive them back, stamped with their visa by return. Unfortunately the Nazis still held their passports. In addition, there were new obstacles that needed to be overcome before the passports would be returned. Departure from Germany would be impossible without clearance from the finance department, the labour exchange and the foreign exchange department. To have any chance of success, Jews would lose most of their worldly possessions.

Under the Decree for the Reporting of Jewish Owned Property, all Jews had to register any property or assets valued at more than 5,000RM (then £400). By early 1939 more than 7 billion RMs' worth of wealth had already been logged, ready for state-sanctioned looting known as 'Aryanisation'.

By 1 January 1939 all Jewish land and firms had to be sold to non-Jews and Jews were forbidden from buying gold, silver, jewellery or art worth more than 1,000RM (then £80). This was followed by a decree requiring the surrender of precious metals and stones in Jewish ownership.

On 31 January the Fehrs were notified by the Third Reich that their application for the return of passports had been denied.

Under the terms of the decree, the Nazis demanded a list of all the family's jewellery, gold, silver, platinum and precious stones. They had a fortnight to hand in these valuables to the state without compensation. Inge noted in her diary that the family were told 'now we know what's here, hand them in.'

Jeanne was indignant. Accompanied by Inge, they visited a small jewellery shop and purchased cheaper versions of the items listed. The inferior items were handed in to the Nazis, while the originals were given to their few loyal Aryan friends to look after on their behalf.

Inge wrote: 'The Nazis had the flawed diamonds and low carat bracelets, our friends had the good jewellery.'

It was a small victory for the Fehrs, but it felt good.

The most valuable items went to Emmy Lignitz, who had been so kind to the family. After the war, the jewellery was returned to the family.

In March, Kitty was offered a place on the Kindertransport (the organised transportation of children without their parents) to travel to the UK on her own. For the past four months, the Refugee Children's Movement (also known as the Kindertransport) had sent representatives into Germany and Austria to transport children at risk into foster homes in the UK. Kitty was not actually Jewish and it was hoped she would assimilate well into a Christian household.

Kitty wrote in her diary: 'I could go to England now and live with a vicar's family. They apparently want to take in a non-Aryan Protestant 15-year-old girl. As I am the only Protestant girl in the class, I am the only one eligible, but I don't want to [go]. I want to stay in Germany for as long as possible.'

However, there was soon better news for the whole family. On 6 April 1939, Oscar was informed by Captain Foley that the British government would allow him to work in the UK, so long as he successfully retook his medical qualifications. This was the best news imaginable and the Fehrs were extraordinarily fortunate given resistance by the British Medical Association to allowing German and Austrian Jewish doctors to practice in the UK.

By 1938, when the situation of Europe's Jews was seen as critical, the Home Secretary Sir Samuel Hoare had wanted to relax the restrictions on Jewish doctors and allow 500 to enter and work in the UK. This plan was scuppered by the self-interest of the BMA, who stated that 'British Medicine had nothing to gain from new blood and much to lose from foreign dilution.'[12] This was despite the fact that German universities had been the most sought-after in the world, with their medical doctors receiving the highest number of Nobel recognitions (forty-one awardees) between 1901 and 1936.[13] Oscar was one of only fifty doctors given a working visa to the UK.

The tense, agonising wait for the return of their passports continued.

When the girls returned to school on 17 April, they were shocked to discover the SS had taken over the building. The school had been moved to a nearby smaller house. As pupils and teachers emigrated, pupil numbers were halved and classes were combined. By the following month, only 245 pupils remained at the school, with sixteen teachers plus three dedicated English teachers who were preparing pupils for the UK school-leaving certificates that summer. Former pupils said they found the daily departure of classmates disruptive, disquieting and a constant reminder of the threat they faced.¹⁴

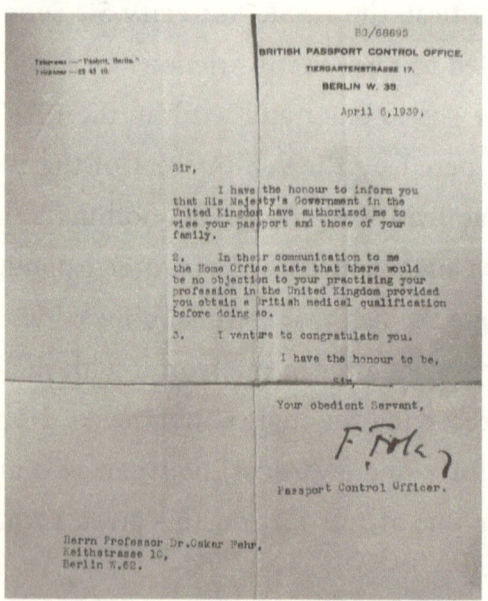

LETTER FROM CAPTAIN FOLEY INFORMING OSCAR
HE WAS OFFERED A WORKING VISA FOR THE UK

In her free time, seventeen-year-old Inge defiantly took enormous risks without telling Kitty or her parents.

Trading on her Aryan looks, she sat on non-Jewish benches, attended the circus, the zoo and walked proudly on main roads. She also made one hugely dangerous and illicit trip to the cinema: 'I had dressed in the clothes which the Hitler Youth had adopted as their off-duty gear, black skirt with a white blouse, and went to a distant part of Berlin to see the film *King of the Vagabonds*. It was the only time I got scared, expecting a search by the SS any moment. I saw my head already on the block. I would not be able to give a false name as they had my fingerprints. I had told no one else at home so that no one but me would suffer if I were caught.'

INGE, 1939

But unbeknown to the family, Kitty too had been taking appalling risks. Hidden among her effects was a tiny notebook in which she collected anti-Nazi jokes. It was a small act of defiance to make her feel better but this too was a capital offence. The book was successfully smuggled into the UK.

FROM KITTY'S LITTLE JOKE BOOK

A Nazi runs over a dog and says to the dog's owner: 'Heil Hitler, the dog is dead'. The dog owner replies 'Thank God.'

Goering falls into the water and three boys save him. He wants to fulfil everyone's wish. The first wants a car, the second a plane and the third a state funeral. Goering asks why. The third boy says: 'If my father hears that I saved you - he will kill me.'

There are three characteristics in the German people: honesty, intelligence and National Socialism. But no German has more than two of them. Either he is honest and intelligent, then he is not a Nazi, or he is a Nazi and honest, then he is not intelligent, or he is a Nazi and intelligent, then he is not honest.

A singer sings songs to Hitler. After singing a series of songs, Hitler asks him if he would like to sing something for him. The Kaddish (sung at funerals), says the Jewish singer.

Inge wrote to her sister more than sixty years later: 'I still shudder to think what would have happened to us, if Nazis had found the tiny notebook in which you had written down the anti-Nazi jokes. The penalty was concentration camp.' This booklet is now housed in the Wiener Holocaust Library in London.

Finally, on 4 July 1939 the family's passports were returned. The Fehrs headed straight to the British Consulate, where they also had to produce their Unbedenklichkeitsbescheinigung, their tax clearance certificate.

Inge wrote: 'In the morning, Papa, Mama and I went to the British Embassy to collect our visas. Captain Foley greeted us in the corridor, invited us into his office and talked with Papa. He said that Papa was the first doctor in six months who received a work permit for England. We are also among the very few people who have been given a permanent residence permit. Afterwards we went to the British travel agency and were given 33 brochures. We spent the evening and night packing our books into suitcases.'

The UK, US and much of Europe would accept only a finite number of refugees. Reports from Cabinet discussions show the UK had not been acting purely out of altruism in accepting some Jewish refugees. If they were to take refugees, they wanted the high-achieving ones: 'It would be in the public interest to try and secure for this country prominent Jews who were being expelled from Germany and who had achieved distinction whether in pure science, applied science such as medicine or technical industry, music or art. This would not only obtain for this country the advantage of their knowledge and experience but would also create a very favourable impression in the world.'[15]

All refugees, including those of the desired 'distinction', still had to show they would not become a drain on national resources. All adults had to demonstrate the ability to support themselves or be sponsored. The

OSCAR'S TAX CLEARANCE CERTIFICATE

COPY

WT/EMC   16th November, 1938.

Dear Sir,

I understand that you have been very kind to my sister, Mrs. Jeanne Fehr who has applied to you for permission to come to England with her family.

I am very anxious that she should have this opportunity and am more than willing to undertake that during their stay in England they will be my guests. I will give any undertaking that may be required that I accept full responsibility for them here.

I am a stockbroker and Member of the London Stock Exchange since 1909 and partner in this firm since 1911.

Mr. G.H.S.Pinsent, C.M.G. of our Embassy in Berlin is personally acquainted with my partner, Sir Herbert Ellissen, O.B.E. and myself, and will no doubt be willing to answer any questions.

I remain,

Yours faithfully,

signed W. Traub

Captain Foley,
British Consulate General,
Thiergartenstrasse,
BERLIN W. Germany.

WILLY TRAUB'S LETTER TO CAPTAIN FOLEY

WILLY WITH JEANNE AS A CHILD

Fehrs were sponsored by Jeanne's brother, Willy Traub, a stockbroker from London, who promised that he would provide for the family on their arrival to the UK.

In total, the UK issued visas to approximately 40,000 Jewish refugees, including 10,000 unaccompanied children on the Kindertransport. Tens of thousands of adults who tried to come to Britain failed.

Elsewhere, the US accepted 95,000 refugees, Palestine 60,000, 75,000 went to Central and South America, Canada 6,000, Australia 10,000, South Africa 6,000. The only destination that did not insist upon visas was Shanghai in Japanese-occupied China, which took 18,000.

By the end of 1939, around 200,000 Jews remained in Germany. By October 1941, when Jewish emigration was forbidden, the number of Jews in Germany had declined to 160,000, nearly all of whom were murdered in concentration camps or ghettos.[16]

Those able to emigrate had to hand over most of their savings and possessions as a condition of being allowed to leave. However wealthy the refugees had once been, they were now unable to support themselves on reaching their destination.

For the Fehr family, now was the time to pack. Their worldly possessions were divided into two - crates to be left in Germany and luggage they would take with them to Britain. Packing was hard work. The family was exhausted, tense and emotional, as Kitty noted in her diary: 'Now everything is in a terrible mess at home, we must sort everything into hand luggage, checked-in luggage and "storage". Mutti is hugely nervous and keeps saying that we're not doing anything when we're working morning till night. For about the last four weeks I haven't made it to bed before one o'clock.'

Once the items had been separated, the rest of the process had to be heavily supervised by officials. Inge reported in her diary: 'The packers came. There were three packers and two customs officers. As he arrived one of the packers warned us "one of the customs officers is a real stinker, but don't worry he's going to leave soon". He was right. At first he was a real stinker. He confiscated everything that had even the slightest bit of silver in it.

'Mutti pulled his leg mercilessly. She said, for example, "When you come to England as a prisoner of war, I will treat you very well." Anyway, he liked her ways, became very friendly with Mutti and suddenly conceded all the confiscated silver such as the ashtray and crystal vases with silver edging.'

The customs officers had failed to appreciate the value of many of the items in the flat. According to Oscar's four-page inventory of the goods to be left behind, they included Persian and Afghan rugs, valuable artworks including etchings by artists such as Rembrandt, Käthe

Kollwitz, who was a patient, and a large bust of Napoleon Bonaparte.

After a week the packing was complete. Four shipping containers of furniture and other possessions were moved into storage in Hamburg, while eleven items of luggage were sealed. The family was forbidden from opening these or buying any new items. This diktat was promptly ignored by Jeanne, who bought herself a seal-skin coat and by Inge, who purchased a leather case and penknife.

STORAGE RECEIPT

On 31 July 1939 it was time to leave their home and their country. The family left Berlin via the main station, known as Lehrter Bahnhof, where they were seen off by friends and relatives. Dedda and Emmy Lignitz were each holding a dachshund, which they would look after. It was a day Kitty would never forget: 'Today we left from Lehrter Bahnhof at ten past six. The farewell was awful. Even before, there was great anxiety as Mutti wasn't quite ready with her things and we were worried that we might miss our train. Mutti hurried me around and scolded me a lot and didn't allow me to go in the kitchen to Deddi with whom I really wanted to be for as long as possible, and when she wouldn't allow it, I started to cry.

'At the station, when we were saying goodbye, Deddi started to cry, so I started crying too, as did Roserie [her best friend]. When the train pulled away, Deddi covered her face with both of her hands and cried, and Roserie ran alongside the train for a bit, and the others waved.'

Inge was more sanguine about the departure: 'Dedda, Roserie and Kitty were in floods of tears . . . and I nearly had a lump in my throat too.'

Dedda would join them in the UK after the war. Roserie, being only half Jewish, survived. Three years later, Joseph Goebbels, the minister of propaganda, would announce that Berlin was 'Judenrein' - cleansed of Jews.

The Fehrs travelled to Hamburg to say goodbye to Oscar's sister, Sara Rosenbacher-Levy and her husband, Jacob. At sixty-one and seventy-two respectively, the couple were among many elderly Jews who took the fateful decision to remain.

August the fourth was departure day from nearby Bremerhaven via the high-speed ocean-liner SS *Bremen*. Before being allowed to board the whole family had to be thoroughly body-searched. A female customs officer demanded Inge and Kitty strip completely and even their long hair had to be unrolled. The only possessions they were allowed on them were a steel watch and 10RM (worth 80p at the time).

Jeanne, still defiant, had successfully concealed a small black pearl.

The girls' emotions were complex. Above all else, Inge was overwhelmed with relief. Kitty was utterly disconsolate at leaving Dedda and their dogs. She commented to her grandson many years later: 'I was very unhappy to leave. I did not realise how lucky we were not only to be leaving as a family but also to be escaping an almost certain unpleasant death.'

While emigration undoubtedly saved their lives, their immediate future was to be a challenging one. In the impending war, not all Britons wanted Germans living in their midst.

CHAPTER 3

THE UK

SS *BREMEN*

While the Fehr family was prevented from taking valuables and cash out of Germany, there was nothing stopping them from leaving their homeland in style. The tickets bought with their remaining German Reichmarks were the best available. The manifest from SS *Bremen* shows that Oscar Israel, Jeanne Sara, Ingeborg Sara and Kitty Sara, as they were now known with their 'Jewish names', had purchased first-class cabins on one of the finest luxury express liners in the world.

The departure of the German super-ship was marked by a grand brass fanfare as the 2,000-plus passengers set sail, travelling in first, second, tourist and third-class comfort. For Inge and Kitty, it was their first sea-borne voyage, their first visit to the UK and the start of a brand-new life. Kitty had been complaining of a stomach ache – she put this down to eating too many fruit lollies – but nervousness, excitement and emotion probably played a role too.

Having set sail for their twenty-five-hour trip, it was time to explore the ship. Both girls were incredibly excited. Kitty observed: 'The ship is great. It has sixteen floors, a lift, a gym, swimming pool, tennis, table tennis, shops, hairdresser, etc. The food was great, you can eat what you want; if you were able to you could eat 102 courses for lunch.'

Inge treated herself to the onboard hairdresser who set her hair in 'finger waves' – a bobbled hairstyle favoured by the Hollywood actresses of the era. It was a huge departure from the waist-length plaits of her childhood.

Their relaxation on board was a brief one. By 4 p.m. the next day, the ship had docked into Southampton. Before the family could leave, customs officials boarded the ship to carry out a thorough inspection of passports and visas.

From Southampton they headed to London. Everything looked and felt so different from Germany. Inge: 'After the Nazi storm troopers, to see British bobbies

SUNDECK RESTAURANT ON SS *BREMEN*

SS *BREMEN*'S SWIMMING POOL

made me feel safe. I was optimistic for a bright future in England.'

Waiting for them among the crowds at Waterloo Station was Jeanne's brother, Willy. He would take care of them in their early days in London and provide initial financial support, since they were only allowed to carry a small amount of pocket money into the country.

The family were also funded by Oscar's son Bob, who was now a successful engineer in the US, and by the Rosenwald family of the Sears, Roebuck and Co. clothing store in the US. The Rosenwalds were known for their charitable giving to Jewish immigrants but they had a particular reason to be generous to Oscar. As a young man he had provided free treatment to a penniless Latvian lady, who had a young daughter, Mary. The girl grew up to be extremely beautiful and an accomplished violinist. She was spotted by the famous American philanthropist William Rosenwald and the couple married in 1938. Grateful for Oscar's kindness to his mother-in-law, William offered Oscar £3,000 over three years to support his family's move to the UK. Inge noted: 'In gratitude to my father for treating his wife's mother without asking for a fee, Mr Rosenwald offered to support us during our immigration. Reluctantly we had to accept this most generous offer. This money would enable Kitty and me to continue with our education, otherwise we would have needed to become domestic servants.'

Willy had booked them into Hotel Fairfax in Holland Park from where they spent the next few days settling in and sightseeing. Formalities began the next day, when the family was instructed to attend the Aliens Registration Office at Bow Street Police Station. They waited in a queue for over five hours before they could be formally registered by the police.

On 15 August there was an emotional reunion for the former pupils of the Goldschmidt Schule who had succeeded in leaving Germany. Inge and Kitty's cousin,

'ALIENS' QUEUING AT BOW STREET POLICE STATION

Annamarie Seelig, was there. She had emigrated the previous year and the three would remain close until Annamarie's death seventy-six years later. The event was also attended by the headteacher Dr Leonore Goldschmidt, who had escaped in July with her family. Her husband, Ernst, had left Germany in 1938, while Leonore had stayed on another year helping most of her pupils escape to the UK under the Kindertransport.

With her mother's permission, finally Kitty was allowed to visit a London hairdresser to have her signature long plaits cut off. Unfortunately, this long-awaited moment was not a success. Whereas the fashion for hair at the time was to be set in curly chin-length bobs, her thick hair never really conformed. She wrote in her diary that rather than looking grown-up, her hair was much too short and she now resembled 'a cross between a monkey and a hairbrush.'

KITTY POST-HAIRCUT

For the family to thrive in the UK, Oscar needed to be able to resume his career. Unfortunately, not only did the British medical elite restrict the number of foreign doctors entering the country, but placed roadblocks in front of them when they arrived. Despite the fact that Oscar had forty-three years' experience treating patients at the highest level, his experience was not recognised in the UK.

The number of foreign degrees accepted for registration by the General Medical Council (GMC) had reduced after 1886, when German university degrees lost their validity in Britain. Medical institutions in the UK were keen to ensure British-born doctors would not lose their jobs to more qualified foreign ones.

In 1942, Lord Dawson, the President of the Royal College of Physicians, would comment 'the number of [foreign doctors] that could usefully be absorbed or teach us anything, could be counted on the fingers of one hand.'[17]

As the war developed, there would be some pressure imposed by politicians, such A.V. Hill, who advocated that overseas doctors could raise standards and help at a time of acute medical need. However, in 1939 and at the grand old age of sixty-eight, the only option for Oscar was to seek a university place to retrain as a doctor. He had expected to use his skills while studying and wrote to the BMA, stating: 'I would be very glad to have the opportunity of showing my gratitude for the reception in your hospitable country' by working for free as an emergency doctor. They did not take him up on his offer.

He had hoped to study at the University of London but was informed that only seven foreign doctors were admitted to the university every year and the quota had already been filled.

He decided to apply to the University of Edinburgh, which had a famous medical department. After informing the police of the move, on 31 August the family took the Flying Scotsman to Edinburgh. The seven-hour journey wasn't pleasant as smoke entered the carriage and the family had no idea what would happen or where they would stay on their arrival. A fellow passenger recommended the Clifton Hotel in Portobello, a suburb of Edinburgh. Kitty reported in her diary that they were kicked out by the landlord after only one night since no Germans were allowed. This was hardly the welcome they had anticipated when they left Bremerhaven.

They had better luck at the Mayfield Hotel in the centre of Edinburgh, where the landlady, Mrs Macrae, took to the family immediately and gave the girls chocolate. Her teenage son, Donald, tried to teach the girls how to play golf in the hotel grounds.

Soon after their arrival, blackout regulations were imposed. These required that all windows and doors should be covered with heavy curtains to prevent any light from escaping at night to help the enemy. Inge and Kitty helped Mrs Macrae to prepare the curtains and to sew up sandbags.

At 11.15 a.m. on 3 September 1939, Prime Minister Neville Chamberlain announced that Britain was at war. As Germans, albeit friendly Germans, the family's movements would be closely monitored.

The Aliens Department of the Home Office was calculating the risk of the 73,000 aliens over the age of sixteen.[18] They were seen as a potential 'enemy within' and were all assessed by special tribunals, which would divide them into three categories, Category A to be interned, Category B to be subject to special restrictions and Category C to be exempt from internment or restrictions. Oscar, Jeanne and Inge were regarded as low risk but were informed they were not allowed to leave Edinburgh and were classed as 'Friendly Enemy Aliens'. As a fifteen-year-old, Kitty was not categorised.

The family would listen to the radio, the most up-to-date source of news, with the rest of the Mayfield guests. On 29 September, after a twenty-eight-day siege of the Polish capital, the fall of Warsaw was announced. Kitty wrote in her diary: 'Today Warsaw had to surrender because it had no more food and water and because the whole of Warsaw was in flames. The radio said that not a single house was whole and that no house was without dead. War is a terrible thing.'

Since the start of the war, the postal service between the UK and Germany had stopped, apart from occasional exchanges through neutral countries or via the military postal service. Communication with friends and family back home was impossible. This upset Kitty immeasurably. She wrote in her diary: 'I would so much like to know how Deddi is. She must surely be an air-raid warden. I don't even know if she is still healthy. I'm not even allowed to write to her. If only I could get news of her and also of Roserie.'

Kitty was quite right not to attempt to contact friends and relatives in Germany. Letters to Germany via third parties were intercepted and some children who had travelled to the UK on the Kindertransport were arrested for attempting to contact their parents and sentenced to immediate internment with adults.[19]

Inge and Kitty enrolled at George Watson's Ladies College on 12 October. Since the girls' school had been taken over for war work, the female pupils shared the boys' college. Their fellow pupils were kind and patient as Kitty reported in her diary: 'My class is terribly nice. I'm in 4a and Inge in 5. The girls help me whenever they

> Our Mystic Language
>
> We go to shoot at grouse
> But never shoot at grouses,
> Yet when we sea a house
> We look at many houses,
> Mother in her blouse
> And sisters in their blouses
> Don't, though they dread a mouse,
> Ask are there any mouses
> We call our mouses mice,
> Yet houses are not hice,
> While grouses are neither
> Grouses nor grice.
>
> Jonette Westwood
> Duddingston 1939

HELP WITH THE ENGLISH LANGUAGE FROM A FELLOW PUPIL

can. We always play air raids here so everyone knows which shelter to go to when things get serious.'

At seventeen and fifteen respectively, Inge and Kitty were at a critical point in their education. Although their English had improved at the Goldschmidt Schule, it was a long way off the required standard. Inge and Kitty did their utmost to catch up.

In Kitty's first term her headteacher wrote: 'Kitty has made a good effort in all her classes, seriously handicapped as she is with the language difficulty.' Her only 'very good' was her conduct.

KITTY AND INGE IN THEIR NEW SCHOOL UNIFORMS

Inge and Kitty made friends at the Rangers, the section for the oldest girls at the Girl Guides, and took part in the national Dig for Victory campaign, introduced by the Ministry for Agriculture, planting fruit and vegetables in allotments and gardens. Their landlady allocated a spot in the hotel garden where they could work. The girls were brimming with enthusiasm and were inspired to do their bit to help the war effort.

THE DIG FOR VICTORY ANTHEM

Dig! Dig! Dig! And your muscles will grow big big big
Keep on pushing spade. Don't mind the worms.
   Just ignore their squirms
And when your back aches laugh with glee
And keep on diggin' til we give our foes a Wiggin'
Dig! Dig! Dig! To Victory.

The Dig for Victory campaign would prove highly successful. In the 1930s, Britain imported 70 per cent of its food, relying on 20 million tonnes of shipping each year. If shipping was disrupted, there would be a risk of severe food shortages. During the war fruit and vegetables were grown not just in gardens and allotments but throughout public spaces, including parks, grass verges on the side of roads, playing fields and cricket greens. By 1945, 75 per cent of food was grown domestically, freeing up shipping for war materials.

By now, German bombing of the city of Edinburgh was frequent. When the air-raid sirens went off the girls would have to rush to the hotel's cellar, and it was here they often worked on their homework by candlelight. With the threat of a possible German invasion, the atmosphere in the city was tense.

When Kitty turned sixteen in December 1939, she went to the police station to get registered: 'I'm the first case in the whole of Edinburgh where a German has turned sixteen after the tribunal, but as the tribunal has already finished, they don't know what to do. I have no idea whether I am an "enemy alien". He [the policeman] didn't think that I looked all that dangerous.'

The family celebrated a traditional German Christmas on 24 December. When it was dark they lit candles on the

KITTY'S ALIEN EXEMPTION FROM INTERNMENT FORM

small tree in Oscar and Jeanne's bedroom. Kitty played *'Stille Nacht'* on her flute and they exchanged small presents. Christmas Day was spent with the other guests in the hotel. The girls quietly lamented the omnipresent turkey, which was served for both lunch and dinner. In Germany, they always had goose.

By spring 1940, Germany seemed unstoppable. The Nazis had invaded Denmark and Norway (April), Holland, Belgium, France and Luxembourg (May). Would the UK fall next?

In Germany new concentration camps were being opened, including the infamous Auschwitz in southern Poland from May 1940.

The Fehrs had no knowledge of what was happening inside Germany and no letters from their friends, family or Dedda. The first information they received concerned their possessions. The Nazis had seized all their belongings which had been carefully stored in four 5-metre crates in the Freihafen (free port) of Hamburg. This was the entire contents of their house, their furniture, paintings and remaining personal effects, including many reels of cinefilm. All these possessions had been auctioned off with the money going to the Nazis. They were not only valuable but held great sentimental value. After the war, Oscar, Inge and Kitty strove for a return of their possessions, to no avail.

Adding insult to injury, Germany had stripped all Jewish refugees of their citizenship. Oscar, Jeanne, Inge and Kitty were now stateless - they were neither German nor British and therefore belonged nowhere. They were soon to realise they had no base in Scotland either.

Edinburgh had become an important military centre with 33,000 British troops based there. It was also close to strategically important airfields and naval bases. The authorities decided it was too risky to have enemy aliens living in the vicinity and so, having originally been told they couldn't leave Edinburgh, the Fehrs were now informed they couldn't stay. In a letter dated 14 June 1940, Oscar was instructed that: 'Notice is hereby given to you, being an alien and being a resident in an area declared to be a Protected Area, are required to take immediate steps to remove [yourself] from this area [within three days].'

The girls were sad and bade tearful goodbyes to the new friends they had made in Rangers just as they had started to settle in. Kitty diaried: 'We have to leave Edinburgh in three days. We went to Rangers today [to say] goodbye. We dug for victory, played and said a fond farewell. Next week we could have done our interpreter and knitter badges.'

One kindly police officer, a Sergeant Peebles, suggested they should move to an attractive town

DARING TO BE

MH

EDINBURGH CITY POLICE

A.26/125

Aliens Department,
Central Police Chambers,
Edinburgh, 1.

14th June, 1940.

Aliens (Protected Areas) Order.

In the present emergency it is necessary to restrict aliens from entering or residing in certain areas adjoining the coasts of Great Britain and in certain other vulnerable areas, and the Secretary of State has accordingly made an Order under the Aliens Order declaring certain areas to be Protected Areas within the meaning of the Aliens Order, 1920. The effect of the Order is that no foreigner can enter into, or reside in, any area declared to be a Protected Area without the written permission of the Chief Constable.

Notice is hereby given to you that you, being an alien and being resident in an area declared to be a Protected Area, are required to take immediate steps to remove from this area, and that if you are found in this area after the expiry of three days from the date of this notice, steps will be taken to enforce the Order against you. You will be allowed to make your own arrangements for leaving the Protected Area, but you must not go to any other aliens Protected Area, nor to any place within 20 miles of the East or South coasts of Great Britain.

After removal from the Protected Area you should, if you desire employment, register with the nearest employment exchange in the district in which you take up your residence.

The only applications for exemption from this prohibition which will be entertained are applications made by or on behalf of persons holding key positions in industries engaged in work of national importance. Any such application should be made forthwith to me at the above-mentioned address, and in the case of an employee the application should be supported by the employer.

Chief Constable.

Oskar Fehr, Esq.,
15 Mayfield Gardens,
EDINBURGH.

'ALIENS' WERE GIVEN THREE DAYS TO LEAVE EDINBURGH

twenty miles away on the River Tweed, which bore his name. So they moved to Peebles where they rented rooms in the Hay Lodge Hotel and informed the police of their arrival.

Yet again, the girls remained positive. They adored the grounds and set about getting to know the other guests - a varied bunch. Kitty wrote: 'It's a fabulous hotel with a garden right on the River Tweed where you can swim and row and there's a big garden with strawberries and vegetables. There are young and old rabbits, cats, dogs, hens and chicks. The people at the hotel are very nice. I've already weeded out the garden a bit. The house is full of children. Brian, a terribly naughty 7½ year old throws other people's things into the water and says "not mine".'

The accommodation was £3 a week to include free baths and four meals a day at 9 a.m., 1.30 p.m., 4 p.m. and 7 p.m.

For Inge and Kitty, the move meant enrolling in yet another school for the last few weeks of the summer term. Peebles High School was their fourth school in three years. Again, their fellow pupils were very kind, albeit amused to hear English spoken in German-Scottish accents.

Meanwhile, with the risk of a German invasion high, concerns over enemy aliens increased. On 25 June 1940

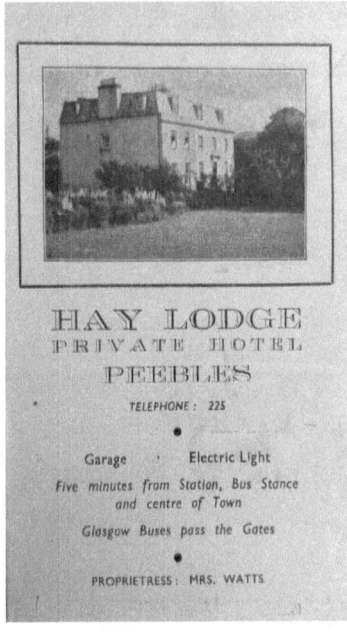

HAY LODGE ADVERT

INGE AND KITTY BEFRIENDED THE OTHER CHILDREN AT THE HOTEL

there was bad news for the family. Kitty wrote: 'In the afternoon I suddenly heard Mutti say to Inge "Papi is being interned." What a shock. I ran out of the room to my mother and asked what was going on. Two officers had been there all afternoon and looked at papers. They found nothing but said they had been ordered to lock up all male foreigners. Papi quickly packed his bags and changed his clothes. We were able to accompany Papi downstairs, where there was a grey private car. Then there was a lot of crying: Mutti, Betty, the parlour maid, Mrs Harrington, Mrs Watts the landlady, Joyce's mother is said to have had tears in her eyes and I couldn't resist it either and cried but nobody saw it.'

The arrest and internment of Oscar had been totally unexpected due to his age. The confinement had no end date and the family had no way of knowing when or if they would see him again. Having escaped one form of persecution, they were now subjected to a second.

> **INTERNMENT**
>
> By 1939 there were assessed to be around 73,000 potential enemy aliens in Britain whom, it was feared, could be hostile to the UK either as spies or by offering assistance to an invading army. In fact, some 55,000 of these were Jewish refugees and therefore hardly likely to be sympathetic to the Nazis.[20]
>
> By February 1940 nearly all the tribunals had completed their work. The vast majority, 66,000 adults, were considered harmless and no restrictions were imposed. Some 6,700 were deemed to require imposition of movement and 569 were seen as requiring internment. Camps were set up around Glasgow, Liverpool, Manchester, Bury, Huyton, Sutton Coldfield, London, Kempton Park, Lingfield, Seaton, Paignton and the Isle of Man.

Tensions mounted in the spring of 1940 following the German invasion of Norway. More and more Germans and Austrians were rounded up. Italians were also considered for internment following Italy's declaration of war on Britain on 10 June 1940.

With 28,000 internees there was a space problem. To ease the overcrowding, more than 7,500 internees were forcibly deported thousands of miles away to Canada and Australia.

Tragically some never returned. On 1 July 1940, the liner *Arandora Star* left for Canada carrying 1,000 German and Italian internees. During the crossing the ship was torpedoed and sunk with the loss of 714 lives, most of them internees.

Some of the survivors from *Arandora* were among the 2,500 transported the following month aboard the hired military transport HMT *Dunera* from Liverpool to Australia. The treatment of these internees was atrocious. They were allowed above deck for just thirty minutes a day over the two-month voyage. With only ten toilets between them, effluent flowed across the decks.

The soldiers beat and abused the men, forcing them for instance to walk barefoot across broken beer bottles. Their documents and possessions were stolen or thrown overboard.[21]

The suffering of these men, on top of the news of the *Arandora*, caused an outcry in parliament, resulting in the first release of internees from British camps in August 1940. By February 1941 more than 10,000 had been freed, and by the following summer, only 5,000 were left in internment camps. For the most part, those released contributed to the war effort and some served in the armed forces.

The US also interned their 'enemy aliens' after the Americans entered the war in December 1941. Some 100,000 Japanese Americans on the west coast were interned, often in very poor conditions.[22] As has been well documented, extremely harsh treatment was meted out to civilians in internment camps by the Germans and Japanese.

So far, the Fehrs had faced their challenges together but without Oscar at her side, Jeanne was bereft. She begged to be allowed to visit Oscar but was turned down.

She wrote to Oscar almost daily, campaigned for his release and sent him parcels - including books, clothes and home-made raspberry jam. She was especially

> D/Int/Visits.
>
> To:-
> Mrs E. Felor,
> Hay Lodge Private Hotel,
> Peebles.
>
> Madam,
>   Referring to your letter of the 27th inst., I regret to inform you that visits to Internees are not allowed.
>
>   Yours faithfully,
>
>   Captain,
>   Adjutant Donaldson's School Camp.
>
> West Coates,
> Edinburgh.
> 28-6-40.

JEANNE WAS REFUSED PERMISSION TO VISIT OSCAR

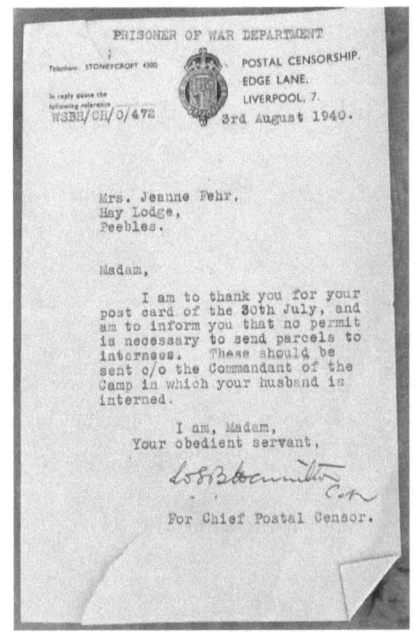

PERMISSION WAS GRANTED TO SEND PARCELS

concerned that the summer clothes he was wearing during his arrest would be totally unsuitable. She wrote shortly after his detention: 'I am violently anxious that you are ill as you only had your very thin things with you and it has got so cold since.' She also kept him updated of the comings and goings in the hotel and the girls' progress:

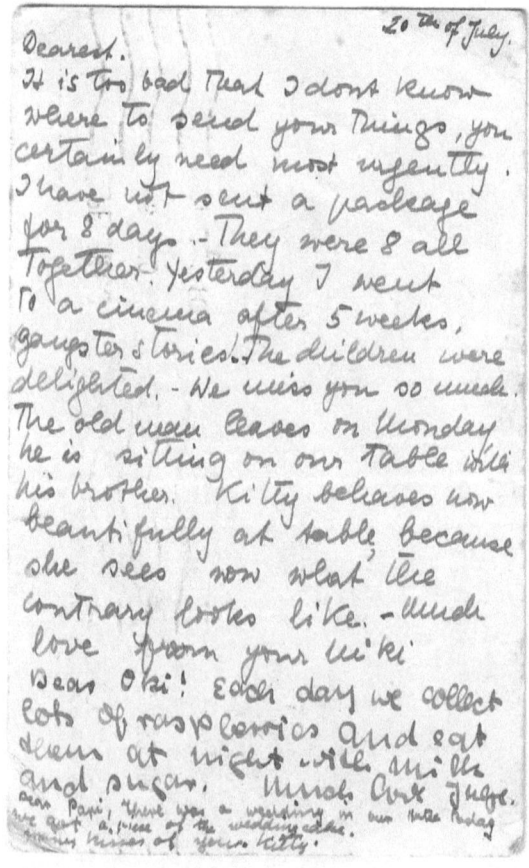

LETTER FROM JEANNE TO OSCAR

'The old man [staying at the hotel] is sitting on our table. Kitty behaves now beautifully at table because she sees what the contrary looks like. Inge looks exceedingly pretty, even Kitty is very tidy just now.'

The girls also wrote regularly to their father. After just a year in the UK, they chose to communicate in nearly fluent English. They tried to cheer him up. Undoubtedly their letters would have been intercepted before reaching him, so the contents were a little banal.

> Dear Papi,
> Just now I have finished to wash the hair of Inge, before I started she put a hair tonic on her hair, which will make it shiny. We made a walk today in the rain, nearly always, it is raining here. We are looking forward to getting you back very soon and so are the nice ladies in our hotel, who are very fond of making your acquaintance.
> Many hugs and much love,
> Yours, Kitty

Oscar was allowed to write twice a week and no letter could be longer than twenty-four lines. Of all his many letters still in our possession, all were exactly twenty-four lines long.

HELEN JOHN

> **HAY LODGE PRIVATE HOTEL,**
> **PEEBLES.**
>
> TELEPHONE: 225.
> TELEGRAMS: HAY LODGE, PEEBLES.
> PROPRIETRIX: MRS. WATTS.
>
> Kitty wanted me to become owner of a new born cat, to save its life but I resisted the temptation...
> Your last letter was of the 9th of July. It is hard that the mail takes such a long time, but probably it can't be helped. —
> Much love from
> your
> Miki

> Dear Papi,
> Just now I have finished to wash the hair of Inge, before I started she put a hair tonic on her hair which will make it shining. We made a walk, to-day in the rain, nearly always it is raining here. Yesterday we made a lovely walk on which we discovered a new raspberry paradise. It is on

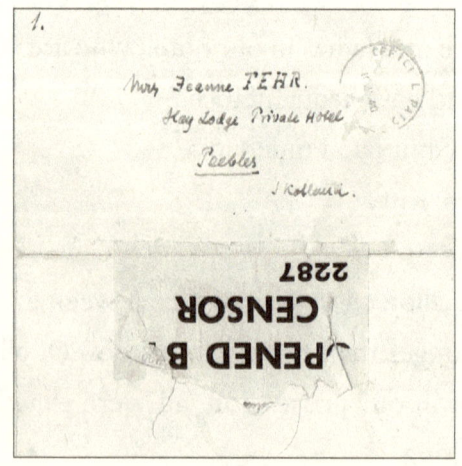

ALL COMMUNICATIONS FROM INTERNS WERE CENSORED

DARING TO BE

> Edinburgh 27. V. 40.
> Donaldson's School Camp.
>
> My dearest Nicki, don't worry about me, I am very well. I was together in our room with 9 fellows from Germany, Austria, Italy and Switzerland. We talked a lot. In the dining room I met S. Schuster and S. Weblau. To-day was medical examination. Because of my old ulcer of stomach, my hernia and also my tendency to collapses I came into the hospital-department, also my room-fellow from Graz, a banker. We met here a very nice people, I can get here a milder food, it is quiet, I can work, and we have beautiful beds. The spitzall is also very nice and gave me a mild treatment. I should like to stay here for longer time, but it is probably that we will be transferred elsewhere earlier or later. I see from our windows of the Arthur seat and all the other hills, where we have been together so many times. I hope you and the children are alright and you enjoy further the beautiful Peebles. Please tell me about the letter of Bob. I did not read it and forgot to take it with me. Wrote him soon. I can't do it, because I am allowed to write a letter only twice a week. The cushion and the plaid and all the other things you put into my bag were very useful for me. — Here I had to interrupt my letter, for it was the time for vacation in the garden. I met D. Sokolka, who is here since yesterday. His wife is still in the Highlands quite alone. I am so happy that the children are with you. I am so longing for you, and Supp, and Kitty. Many kindest regards to all the kind ladies of the hotel. All my love to you 3 and many, many kisses
>
> Yours Oscar.

OSCAR'S LETTER TO HIS FAMILY

At first, he had been placed into Donaldson Camp, near Edinburgh, in a stark Victorian building which had served as a children's hospital. Here he shared a room with nine men of different nationalities.

Oscar underwent a medical examination and, due to an old hernia and a gastric ulcer, was placed in the hospital wing. An unexpected upside of the camp was the reunions with both relatives and friends. He met his cousin, Walter Herz, and many other doctor friends.

Nine days later, Oscar, together with many other internees, was moved to the notorious Warth Mills Camp, near Bury, Manchester. The former cotton factory was a squalid rat-infested environment with scarce water, minimal food and poor sanitation. Internees were strip-searched and had valuables confiscated before being given a blanket and some hay to sleep on.

WARTH MILLS

OSCAR'S SKETCH OF LIFE AT WARTH MILLS

Fellow internee Joe Pieri reported later, 'It was like something out of Dickens: broken glass, dust in the air from the old mills that had been there and broken machinery.' Sanitary conditions were inadequate, lavatories were hastily dug latrines and food was sparse, with no proper rationing system to ensure every man got his fair share.[23]

Oscar never let on to his family at the time about just how bad things were.

On 19 July, a month later, 700 of the 1,800 internees boarded a special train from Liverpool to a new internment centre, Hutchinson Camp on the Isle of Man. They were marched in long columns, accompanied by soldiers, to identical houses for twenty prisoners each. Most men had to share double beds but Oscar pleaded for a single one and was placed in a twin-bedded garret with Dr Martin Zade, an eye specialist from Heidelberg. The men were to become firm friends.

Unlike Warth Mills, Hutchinson Camp had lax restrictions with relatively plentiful food. Inmates were permitted to write two letters per week, play sport and form a camp newspaper. Hutchinson developed a reputation as an artists' colony due to the thriving creative interests of the internees. A famous string quartet, later known as Amadeus, was founded at the camp by four young Austrian-Jewish violinists. After the war they went on to become one of the highest regarded quartets in Europe for forty years. There were cultural and intellectual internees keen to expand their knowledge and interests. Inge noted: 'A culture board had been formed and lectures were held in the open air. My father gave one lecture lasting 1.5 hours, which needed days of preparation. His spare time he spent studying pathology.'

Many of the internees would go on to achieve great things. Some would be professors, politicians, journalists, architects, designers, artists, sculptors, inventors, musical directors, concert pianists, engineers, diplomats, high court judges and lawyers. Arthur Kuranda became an Olympic skier, Oscar Gugen cofounded the British Sub-Aqua Club and many others, like twenty-two-year-old

SKETCH OF ONE OF HIS COLLEAGUES STUDYING - MARTIN ZADE, WHO WAS ALSO A PROFESSOR OF OPHTHALMOLOGY AND HAD WORKED IN BERLIN

OSCAR'S DEPICTION OF TALKS WITHIN THE CAMP

VIEW OF THE EXTERIOR

Hans Arenstein, died fighting for Britain during the Normandy invasion.

Oscar was appointed chief eye specialist for all five internment camps on the Isle of Man. Most mornings he left with the camp commander to tour them, examining patients as well as those of the pioneer corps. Three times a week he held clinics in his own camp. His spare time was spent improving his English, swimming, playing golf, walking and sketching.

While the interns made the most of their lot, they missed their families and loved ones. Any immediate contact, however, would be strictly punished. Intern Kurt Bohm, at twenty-three years old, was sent to solitary confinement for passing his fiancée a flower through barbed wire, and Arthur Tittinger was fined £3 for speaking to his wife through the fence.[24]

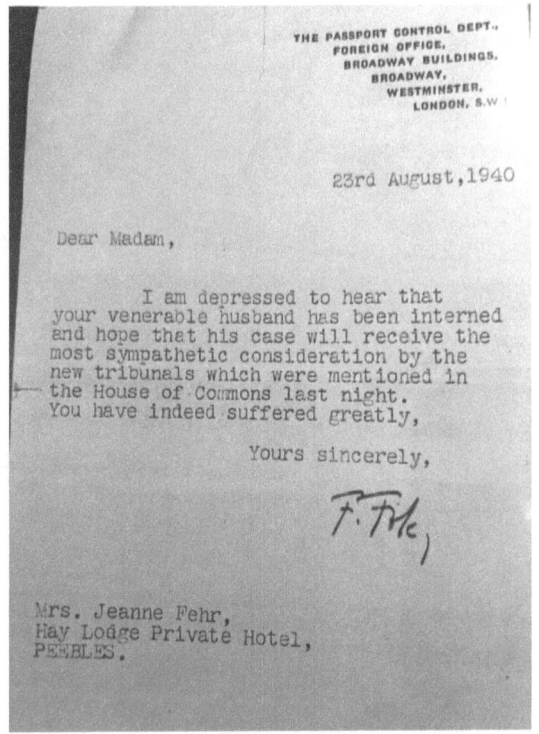

LETTER FROM CAPTAIN FOLEY TO JEANNE

Oscar, however, didn't have too long to wait. Captain Frank Foley had become personally involved in helping Jeanne secure her husband's release. He wrote to her in August expressing his dismay that her 'venerable husband' had been interned and sympathised with her suffering. In the meantime, he personally visited Oscar in the Isle of Man and shortly afterwards the camp commander informed Jeanne that an old age clause had been adopted and her husband would be home soon.

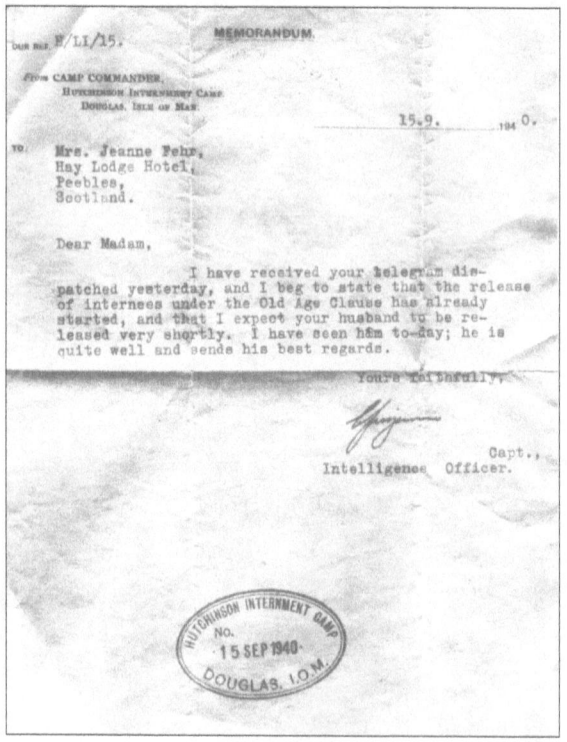

CAMP COMMANDER TELLS JEANNE THAT OSCAR WILL BE RELEASED SOON

Jeanne was overjoyed. As can be seen from her letters she adored and idolised her husband: 'Hurray all men over 65 are to be released - so said the news tonight. But naturally, I prefer that you are released not only for that but because of who you are. On account of your fame, your skill, your experience and for all you can do for mankind up to now and can still do . . . ' The girls not only missed their father dreadfully but were frustrated that he was thwarted from contributing to the war effort.

The happy anticipation of Oscar's release was dashed by some other unexpected news, diaried by Kitty: 'Mrs Watts, the landlady, came in that evening and started apologising ten times, but she wanted us to leave. We pretty much froze into pillars of salt and asked why. She said it wasn't her fault, but two people with a child had said they wouldn't come here while the "Germans" were still there because we were spoiling the atmosphere.'

Another family at the hotel had complained about living under the same roof as German refugees, stating, 'The only good Germans are dead Germans.'

The girls tried to understand why refugees were disliked so much. Kitty reported on one of the reasons she was given: 'Because we grew up in Germany and therefore lived under the Nazis, we must have acquired Nazi characteristics.'

The comment to her was so illogical and so baffling, she didn't know how to respond.

For the next three weeks, Jeanne and the girls scoured the area for alternative accommodation, but there was nothing. Wartime bombing had created a housing crisis, with families moving out of the big cities, while German refugees were not at the top of the list among landlords. Kitty reported that the situation was 'hopeless'.

Oscar was released on 19 September 1940 after a total of two months of internment. Kitty wrote: 'Inge and I

BLACK BARONY

ran out, just as we got to the orchard, the door opens and sure enough, Papi comes. We are happy now. Mummy and Daddy were both crying with joy.'

Due to the lack of accommodation in Peebles, the family moved four miles away into sixteenth-century Barony Castle, known as 'Black Barony', which had been converted into a hotel, and was now home to several refugee families. It was situated in Eddleston and lay in a glorious 80-acre park. With their shared loved for the outdoors this was heaven to Oscar and Kitty in particular. The girls gave their father an oil-painting set - he had a talent for painting, something he hadn't had time for since his youth.

It was amidst the majestic landscape of Black Barony that they celebrated their second Christmas

OSCAR FOUND COMFORT IN PAINTING

OSCAR'S SKETCH OF THE GROUNDS OF BLACK BARONY

since leaving Germany. By now, they had all become fluent English speakers, made new friendships and as far as the war would allow, were actively planning for the future. They were spending too much of their dwindling resources but for now they were together in beautiful, peaceful surroundings.

INGE WITH BLACK BARONY IN THE BACKGROUND

In 1941 Oscar was finally allowed to attend the University of Edinburgh to study and sit his medical examinations. By special permission, he was permitted to travel daily the twenty miles into Edinburgh. Oscar took his first exam in October 1941 and his second six months later.

Inge noted: 'It is not an easy task for an elderly eye-specialist to pass examinations in subjects such as midwifery, forensic medicine, etc in what was still a foreign language for him.'

The girls also studied hard at school, immersing themselves in the English language.

* * *

An unexpected challenge facing the Fehrs was the rise of antisemitism in the UK during the war years. Documents released in 2021 show that British government officials were repeatedly warned about this, but chose not to intervene.[25] Cyril Radcliffe, the director general of the Ministry of Information blamed the Jews themselves for this by displaying 'a lack of pleasant standards of conduct as evacuees'. As food was restricted, Jews were blamed for hoarding and conspiracy theories raged.

This antisemitism was especially marked upon Polish army officers in the UK. This matter was raised in Parliament by Mr Driberg MP for Maldon:

It is with considerable reluctance that I raise to-day, and raised yesterday at Question Time, the problem of anti-Semitism in the Polish Forces in this country ... Of the existence of this sentiment to a pretty wide degree in the Polish Forces, there is no doubt. I know of it from my own experience. I have during this war met quite a large number of Polish officers, in officers' messes and so on, and extremely gallant, charming, and decent young men they are. But, unfortunately, if one gets on to these awkward subjects – which one naturally tries to avoid if one is talking to them – one finds that they have certain fixed prejudices, one of which is this deep prejudice against the Jews. I have seen it in almost all the Polish officers I have met and talked to.[26]

After Poland fell to the Nazis by July 1940 there were 17,000 Polish soldiers in Britain, with many based in East Lothian for tank training. Inge and Kitty would regularly encounter Polish officers. Some of them were charming and came back for tea with the family but there was overt hostility from others. On one occasion, the girls were told to leave a dance they had been looking forward to. Inge wrote: 'We were asked to leave by the Polish officers present because they said we were Germans but really it was because they knew we were non-Aryans.'

This was not only humiliating but hugely disappointing to know that such discrimination had followed them.

Although such incidents were hurtful, the girls had developed thick skins and threw themselves into the wartime effort. They helped to raise money to make Spitfires. At a fundraiser at Black Barony, Jeanne and Inge performed magic tricks while Kitty played the flute. She was an enthusiastic rather than an accomplished musician.

They had fire-fighting lessons, learning how to put out fires with portable stirrup pumps. With their fellow Rangers, they became messengers for the Home Guard and were given armbands marked with the words 'Emergency Relief Organisation'. The role of the Home Guard, comprised mostly of those who were too old or young to fight, was to try to slow the advance of the enemy and protect communication routes from being blocked by them.

The local Girl Guides promise was changed for Inge and Kitty. Instead of promising to do their best 'to God and King', this was amended to 'the country in which I am' - lest they should be loyal to a different king.

Under the terms of the Aliens Restriction Act, the family was banned from owning a car, airplane, motorcycle, signalling devices, telephone or carrier pigeons. While none of this was problematic, they were also not allowed to own a camera, maps or even a bicycle, which might have been convenient.²⁷

The threat presented by the Germans at that point seemed very real. Bombs fell nearby as they left a Rangers meeting on the night of 19 March 1941 with three fires burning around them. More air raids followed over the following weeks.

Inge wrote: 'I just looked out of the windows and saw a land mine explode. There were also 10 other bombs. The house shook, windows rattled. I heard German planes all night and anti-aircraft guns. I watched searchlights moving across the sky. We found a giant crater the next morning, 1 km away, a dead sheep lay next to it killed by the mine. We found 150 pieces of the mine, part of the parachute and rope.'

By April 1941, Germany had invaded Yugoslavia and Greece. In June, Hitler launched Operation Barbarossa - the invasion of the Soviet Union. The fear for the Fehr family was not only the threat of defeat but the possible establishment of a Nazi regime in their new homeland. Inge noted: 'My mother was very much afraid that Hitler would win and that would be the end of us. He had success after success in the beginning. Kitty and I were more optimistic.'

The family also had serious money worries. Without having passed his medical exams, Oscar couldn't work.

By October 1941, the funding from the Rosenwalds was nearly exhausted. They were forced to leave Black Barony once it was requisitioned to house the headquarters for the Polish Higher Military School and needed to find cheaper accommodation.

They rented a remote cottage a mile out of Eddleston. It had neither gas nor electricity and as winter approached, the temperature inside was unbearably cold. Many years later, Kitty described to her family the intense physical discomfort of having to get up in the morning in a freezing cottage. The first job of the day was to light the fire. They developed painful chilblains, giving them swollen and blistered hands and feet.

They endured Christmas in the cottage before moving to a modern flat in Peebles in the new year. The flat had

THE JOY OF ELECTRICITY. JEANNE, INGE AND KITTY READING IN THE FLAT. SKETCH BY OSCAR

three rooms and a kitchen. Although Jeanne complained that she wasn't able to make it feel homely, they were thrilled to be connected to gas and electricity.

Later that year, there came terrible news from Germany. They were informed of the death of their relative, Dr Albert Katzenellenbogen, who had been a prominent barrister and the chair of one of the major banks in Frankfurt. He died in the Maly Trostenets extermination camp in Belarus in August 1942. At this point the Nazis were using gas vans to murder their prisoners. His daughter Grete died as a forced labourer in Frankfurt.

The mass murder of Jews had started in 1941 with mobile killing units pursuing Jews across the occupied territories. In the second phase from 1942, Jewish victims were sent on death trains to centralised extermination camps built for the purpose of the systematic murder of Jews.

The Fehrs were also informed that Oscar's sister, Sarah Rosenbacher-Levy and her husband, Jacob, had died. They were the last relatives they had seen before leaving Germany. The couple had gassed themselves the night before they were due to be deported to Theresienstadt concentration camp.

At home, Jeanne began to feel unwell and was cared for by Inge, who also undertook all domestic tasks,

THE GIRLS WITH JEANNE SHORTLY BEFORE SHE BECAME BED-BOUND

while Kitty finished her last year at school. Jeanne was feeling weary, depressed and irritated by the standard of the housework: 'Inge is still helping in the household. She is extremely quick and does not like to bother about the details.'

Jeanne's illness continued and deteriorated. For a long while Jeanne resisted Oscar's attempts to be examined by a doctor in the hope that she would get better on her own. When, in October 1942, she finally consented, she was examined under anaesthetic at a hospital in Edinburgh. Oscar was informed that his wife had incurable uterine cancer.

Jeanne became weaker and thinner by the day.

On 11 December Kitty wrote: 'Papi fed her tea this morning, Mutti kept reaching past the cup and from then slurred her words and stared blankly into space. Papi said we should prepare ourselves for the worst. She died soon after.'

Jeanne had been oblivious to her plight and had been looking forward to making a full recovery.

Oscar wrote to his cousin Alice: 'My only comfort was that she had not to suffer pain and I could conceal from her the true nature of the disease. So she remained hopeful and cheerful until the last day. It was a cruel constraint to show her always a confident face knowing that there was no hope. I could not tell the truth to the children for she would ask them and the girls cannot lie. I was right, she asked them to tell her what Papi had said about her illness. They answered that she would recover and become healthy again.'

Five days after Jeanne's death it was Kitty's nineteenth birthday. 'I received my first present without Mutti, who had ordered Papi to buy me a George Watson school scarf before she died. So I had something from Mutti too. It hadn't occurred to her that she wouldn't be there for my birthday.'

The following week was a very sombre Christmas in their Peebles flat. They didn't bother with a Christmas

FUNERAL CARD BY THE GIRLS

tree or candles. The girls gave their father a hand-knitted hot-water bottle cover and a framed photo of their mother. Despite the nineteen-year age gap, Oscar and Jeanne had had a very close and loving relationship.

Oscar had no time to grieve. Within a fortnight of his wife's death, he had to sit the second stage of his three examinations. Kitty wrote: 'Poor Papi has never really had time to prepare and he has to sit, I think three written, three oral and three practical exams, which take about 14 days.'

Oscar had forgotten about the time limit for examinations. He wrote at length in response to the first question, only realising too late that he was out of time for the remaining paper. Kitty noted: 'This depressed him and he took a sedative and laid down for a short rest before the afternoon examinations started. He fell asleep and over-slept. In spite of the fact that my father was 30 minutes late, the invigilator permitted him into the examination room.'

Oscar was notified by post that while he had passed medical jurisprudence and public health, he had failed medicine, surgery, midwifery and gynaecology. The girls observed that he was very depressed.

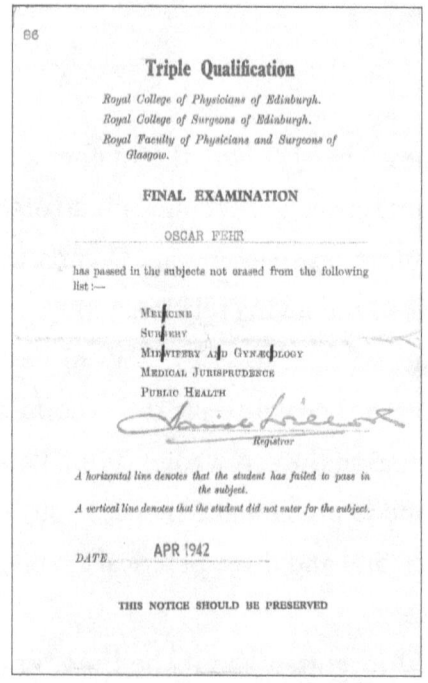

LIST OF CATEGORIES PASSED AND FAILED

In February the family was given permission to move to Glasgow, where Oscar enrolled at the university to re-sit his medical exams. Again, the girls had to say goodbye to their friends and were surprised that many people were so sad to see them leave. Having felt outsiders for so long, it was quite a revelation to them that they were actually well-liked and respected. Kitty diarised: 'At Rangers the Captain made a very nice speech and said how sorry she was that Inge and I had to leave and that we had been such very good Rangers and she thanked us for everything we had done for the Company. I don't know what that could have been.'

In Glasgow, since both girls had graduated from school passing their Scottish Highers, they were expected to contribute to the war effort. Inge was given the choice between the land army, factory work and nursing - she chose the latter. Now twenty-one, Inge left the hotel where her father and sister were staying for a live-in job as a probationary nurse at Redlands Hospital, a private women's hospital staffed entirely by women. She would have one day off a month and half a day off a week for £2 a month. Since she had to share a room with three other nurses, one of whom was on night shift, she was banned from the room in daytime. 'A nurse told me the work was "murder" and she was right. I had to work very hard from 7am to 9pm with two hours off duty.'

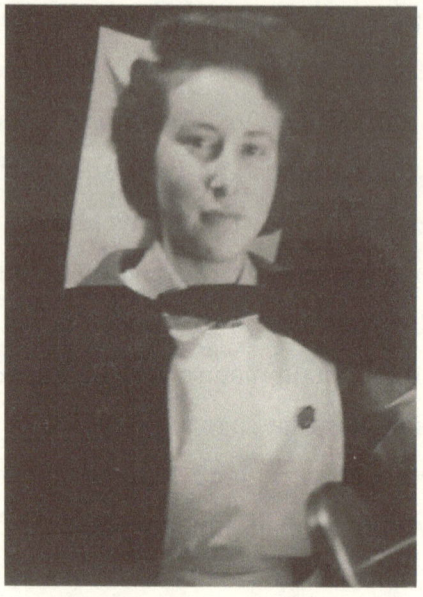

INGE IN HER NEW NURSE'S UNIFORM

As a junior nurse, Inge also had to serve lunch. Only when everyone had eaten could they start lunch themselves but, however hungry they were, they had to stop eating once the matron and sister had finished.

Since Kitty intended to go to university, she had to visit the labour exchange to receive exemption from full-time work and was a part-time cleaner in the maternity unit. She didn't mind the work and found her colleagues friendly. Although she had ambitions to study medicine, a careers adviser at the University of Glasgow tried to dissuade her on the basis that there was 'still prejudice against female physicians'.

Oscar, now aged seventy-two, tried again to pass the remaining three modules. He stayed at the university, studying late into the night. He liked oral exams best. During one examination, he was asked about the dangers of short-sightedness. Inge wrote: 'My father discussed the treatment of detached retinas at some length. After a while the examiners thanked my father for the most interesting discourse but remarked that they were supposed to test him and not be taught by him.'

When the result was announced, Oscar could not contain his excitement - he needed to let the girls know immediately and sent a telegram saying he had 'happily passed'.

After this good news Oscar received two official letters. The first was from the British Medical Association

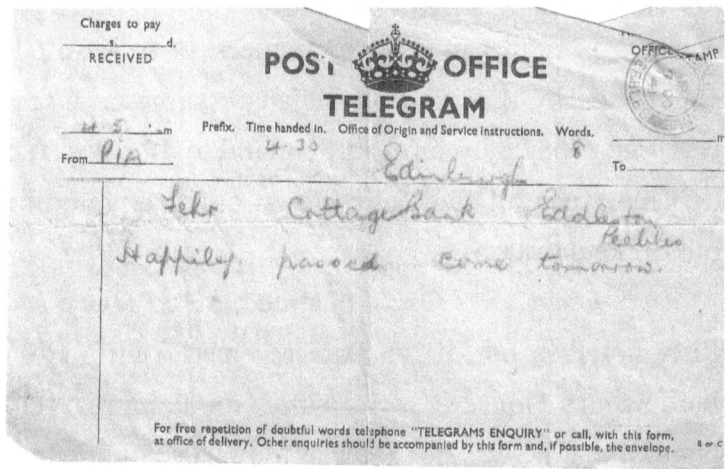

TRIUMPHANT TELEGRAM!

welcoming him into the ranks of the British medical profession. The second came from the Central Office of Refugees. They apparently now recognised the value of medical students from Germany and Austria and wanted to issue them with temporary medical registrations to treat the sick and injured in UK hospitals. They needed Oscar to be on the panel of German-speaking doctors and academics to assess these nearly qualified doctors. Unlike Oscar, these young men (nearly always men) would be spared the challenges of sitting medical exams in a foreign language before being allowed to work.

Having qualified as a doctor for the second time, there were still challenges facing Oscar. The Aliens Committee, which had been advising the Home Office on employment questions of refugee physicians since 1941, stipulated that suitably qualified refugees should work as assistants in private practices, or in hospitals supervised by a British physician or surgeon. Oscar was told repeatedly both in Scotland and in England that his dream of starting his own practice would be out of the question.

Two weeks after Oscar qualified, on 27 May 1943, Kitty noted in her diary: 'Papi received a letter from Bloomsbury House (Central Office for Refugees) telling him that he was not allowed to practise in London: he was allowed to work in the hospital but not to open private practice. Papi is terribly depressed, he was sure he would get permission. He will now apply to be allowed to practise in Glasgow.'

The following week there was more bad news as Kitty diarised: 'Papi went to the Western Eye Infirmary to talk to Professor [Arnold] Löwenstein and others about the prospect of being allowed to practise here. They think it is out of the question that Papi will be admitted here, the Scottish doctors are said to be even worse than the English ones. Yes, the dear colleagues!!!! However, Professor Löwenstein thinks it is likely that a practice will open up soon of its own accord if Papi works at a clinic in London. Papi has decided to go to London. We want to go on Saturday.'

CHAPTER 4

THE LONDON YEARS

The Fehrs moved to a 59-bedroom Victorian boarding house at 4 Adamson Road, Hampstead, London. The home was run by two German refugees, Mrs Lily Sachs and Mrs Bertha Pick, and their long-term guests were predominantly German and Austrian refugees, including several of Oscar's former patients. Mrs Pick had run a successful sanitorium in Bavaria and a boarding house in Berlin. She oversaw the business and food while Mrs Sachs handled the social side. For the refugees who had been through so much, Adamson Road was a safe haven. They were with others who had endured similar trauma. The manageress was Margaret Jacobi, who cared deeply about the residents and was referred to as *Muttchen* - little mother.

Mrs Pick's grandson, Robert, remembers the boarding house as being 'a little piece of Germany' with guests speaking German and where possible, being served German and Austrian food. It would be Oscar's home for the rest of his life. He told his cousin many years later that it had been his dream to have his own flat but he no longer owned anything to put in it.

Oscar started working for free for Moorfields Eye Hospital. Meanwhile those who knew of his work lobbied hard on his behalf. These included Sir Stewart Duke-Elder, a highly acclaimed ophthalmologist and author, as well as other leading consultants.

The Home Office relented to pressure, with Oscar becoming one of a tiny number of refugee doctors to start their own practice.[28] On 28 July 1943, he opened his doors to patients at a consulting room at 81 Harley Street. Two mornings a week he continued to work for free at Moorfields Eye Hospital. His reputation spread quickly, as it had in Berlin. His patients included Dr Chaim Weizmann, the future first president of Israel, whom he operated on twice for cataracts, Philippe Baron de

OSCAR OUTSIDE THE BOARDING HOUSE

Rothschild, a racing driver, author Boris Pasternak and theologian Dr Leo Baeck, who had once been hidden by Frank Foley in Berlin.

In August, Inge began her nursing training at St Helier Hospital in Sutton, South London. Again, this was a live-in position but unlike Redlands it was a brand-new hospital and Inge was treated to a single room of her own. Among her toughest duties was the treatment

OSCAR'S HARLEY STREET SURGERY

of babies and children burned by explosions from the German bombing of London.

'There was an air-raid during the night of February 24th; we admitted two badly burned children, a baby still in his carry cot into which an incendiary bomb had fallen. The blankets and the sheets were charred, the baby had severe burns on both his legs. The other child, a girl of 5, was so badly burned, she only lived until morning.'

By the summer of 1944 the hospital was under threat from the German pilotless planes, or doodlebugs. They made tearing, rasping sounds as they flew but became eerily silent when they dropped with deadly effect. Inge wrote: 'Flying bombs were coming over day and night. Their engines cut off and shortly afterwards they crashed.'

When the bell for danger rang out, doctors and nurses would take cover in the corridors, while protecting patients as best they could. On 22 June a doodlebug hit the hospital grounds opposite the nurses' home. While Inge was only mildly injured by broken glass, many of her colleagues were wheeled into the operating theatre throughout the day with one of them losing an eye.

Five days later, Inge was coming off shift at 9 p.m. when a doodlebug crashed onto the hospital roof. She had called the lift but then changed her mind and was walking down the stairs. 'The lift I had nearly taken, crashed from the fourth floor down into the basement. I could scarcely see or breathe for smoke.'

The whole area was devastated by flying bombs to the extent that 90 per cent of the homes were damaged or destroyed.

Throughout this period Inge was managing to visit Oscar and Kitty, staying overnight with them a day a week. While Inge's life was scary but exciting, Kitty's was less so. She was allowed to work in an industry deemed essential for the war effort, and so the Aliens Department issued her with a restricted permit for work with the British Oxygen Company. She was one of nineteen lab workers, filling flasks with purified helium in a blacked-out garage. She didn't know at the time that the gases would probably have been used by airships, for the tyres of long-range fighter planes and for barrage balloons to protect cities from low-flying enemy aircraft. The work was painstaking, and any leak would contaminate the batch. Kitty was paid £2-18-6 a week. She liked her colleagues and enjoyed socialising in the canteen and playing darts.

In the evenings and weekends she studied at Birkbeck College to achieve her preliminary Bachelor of Science qualification, which would give her the option to study medicine.

Life settled into a routine, albeit with intermittent nightly bombing in what became known as the Baby

INGE ON A VISIT TO ADAMSON ROAD TO SEE OSCAR AND KITTY

KITTY (SECOND RIGHT, WITH HER CO-WORKERS AT BOC)

Blitz. This was the last strategic bombing campaign by the Luftwaffe aimed at Greater London. The RAF Fighter Command enjoyed greatly improved technology to track and destroy bombers and prevent the attacks. The tide of the war was changing.

By 1945 the residents of the Hampstead guesthouse would gather in the lounge to listen to the wireless. The news was increasingly optimistic and when it was reported on 1 May that Hitler had committed suicide in his underground bunker, the residents were ecstatic.

On 7 May, Inge was off-duty. She and her boyfriend, a soldier with an injured arm, gathered with the crowds in Piccadilly Circus. There were crowds and flags as far as the eye could see. The newspaper sellers were rationing newspapers. 'The seller didn't have enough copies and chose who could buy. My friend was in uniform with his arm in a sling. The paperman said "let our wounded hero have one", not knowing that Jim had broken his arm fixing a light bulb.'

Victory in Europe was declared on 8 May 1945. Inge celebrated at the hospital, while Oscar and Kitty heard the news in the boarding house. At the stroke of 3 p.m. a 'ceasefire' was sounded by bugle and the Speaker of the House of Commons introduced Winston Churchill on the wireless declaring victory against tyranny: 'My dear friends, this is your hour. This is not victory of a party

VE DAY IN LONDON

or of any class. It's a victory of the great British nation as a whole.'

After his speech, church bells rang out in every direction. Union Jacks hung from every building. The collective joy was irrepressible. Britain had won the war and Oscar, Inge and Kitty were finally safe.

The extent of the atrocities against Jews finally came to light. The Nazi regime had murdered six million Jewish men, women and children by gassing, shooting, starvation and other means. Two thirds of Europe's pre-war Jewish population had died.

Many of the girls' classmates from the Goldschmidt Schule had successfully escaped to the UK or the US, but others who remained had been deported to concentration camps.

Stripped of their German nationality but still regarded as 'aliens' by their hosts, the Fehr family started the lengthy process of applying to become British citizens. Having submitted extensive paperwork, their three applications were then advertised twice in local newspapers with the request that 'Any person who knows any reason why nationalisation should not be granted should send a written and signed statement of the facts to the Under Secretary of State at the Home Office.' No such objections followed, and the certificates of nationalisation were issued. Inge wrote: 'On October 26th 1947, I went to the police in Bethnal Green to hand in my Alien's Certificate, then went to the Food Office for my new identity card. I was British at last.'

* * *

A few years later, armed with their new British passports and full of trepidation, Inge and Kitty returned to their homeland for a visit. The Tiergarten, the beautiful park by their old home, was now a wasteland - the people of Berlin had cut down the trees to use as firewood during the war. In the zoo cages, where there had once been exotic animals, local people were growing vegetables. They found the street where their apartment had once been - the building had been destroyed and the area was

KEITHSTRASSE IN RUINS 1944

KEITHSTRASSE 1954

unrecognisable to them. It was one of more than 600,000 apartments bombed during the war. Of the city's original population of 4.3 million, there were now only 2.8 million people; and of the 160,000 Jews who had been living in Berlin in 1933, only 1,000 remained.[29] After wandering through the unfamiliar streets, Inge and Kitty picked up the phone book to look for relatives and people they might know - they found no one. People and places were no longer familiar to them. They were tourists in Berlin.

EPILOGUE
WHAT HAPPENED NEXT

DEDDA (VALESKA BUCHHOLZ NEE KONIG)

Dedda did not want to work for another family once the Fehrs had escaped to the UK. She agreed to marry a former employee, Rudi Buchholz, whom the girls had disliked for his heavy drinking and rudeness.

Rudi found a job as a caretaker in an apartment block but was conscripted into the army once the war started. In March 1943, with her husband away, Dedda was approached by a Jewish couple, Mr and Mrs Brieger, who had lived in the same apartment block. The couple, who were listed for deportation the next day, threatened to commit suicide by throwing themselves into the Landwehr Canal. Dedda took them in, concealed them in the annex to her caretaker's lodging, and shared her scant food rations with them. Had she been found out, she would have been deported to a concentration camp or executed immediately. When Rudi learnt what was happening, he was unable to keep his mouth shut. He drunkenly disclosed to his drinking friends 'Meine

Frau hat Juden versteckt' (my wife has concealed Jews). Even though word reached his fellow soldiers, mercifully Dedda was not reported to the authorities. On 23 November 1943, when the building was bombed and set ablaze, Dedda found the Briegers alternative accommodation and they survived the war.

After the war, Dedda followed the Fehrs to London. She remained a close friend until her death in 1970 at the age of seventy-four. She always belittled her bravery, saying, 'Don't fuss, anyone would have done the same.' Inge campaigned for Dedda's courage to be recognised. On 29 March 1984, Yad Vashem, Israel's official memorial to victims of the Holocaust, recognised Valeska Buchholz as Righteous Among the Nations and a tree was planted in her honour.

VALESKA - 'DEDDA'

OSCAR FEHR

In April 1948, having been issued with his British passport, Oscar left with Inge for a sea crossing to New York City to visit his son Bob, whom he hadn't seen since before the war. Bob was now a Doctor of Engineering and introduced Oscar to his wife, Edith, a chemist. It was also an opportunity to reunite with eight of Oscar's former colleagues who had fled to the US. His former chief assistant, Dr Wolffe, held a party in his honour. It was an emotional reunion for all.

Back home, Oscar's clinic in Harley Street was full with old patients and new ones. We found dozens of letters from patients around the world updating Oscar on their family news and thanking him for the gift of sight restored. He was hugely respected in his field, even at the age of eighty-one, and was a key speaker at international medical conferences on advances in ophthalmology. Blessed with good health and vigour, he continued to operate until his eighties.

Following on from the success with the oil paints given to him at Black Barony, he became an accomplished amateur artist. He continued to live at the boarding house in Hampstead, a short walk to the heath, where he loved to paint landscapes. He was a doting grandfather to Inge's three boys. During Kitty's weekend visits, they kept up the family tradition of walks in the countryside.

HELEN JOHN

OSCAR AT A REUNION WITH MANY OF HIS FORMER
COLLEAGUES FROM BERLIN IN NEW YORK, 1948

WITH JOHN AND MICHAEL

OSCAR CONTINUED TO WORK
UNTIL HIS EIGHTIES

Tragedy struck in August 1954 when Oscar suffered a heart attack, followed by a second one six months later. As a result of repeated retinal haemorrhages, he gradually lost all but his peripheral vision. Despite this bitter irony, he kept his spirits up as friends and family visited him, reading from his favourite books.

In 1956, on the fiftieth anniversary of the founding of the Rudolf Virchow Hospital, his achievements were honoured in a celebration ceremony. Oscar was too frail to attend.

In his birthplace, Brunswick, Lower Saxony, a street was named after him – Oscar-Fehr-Weg.

Oscar died in 1959, aged eighty-seven.

Since 2016, the prestigious Oscar Fehr lecture has been held every two years at the meeting of the German Ophthalmology Society in Berlin. It is billed as 'a testament to the resilience, integrity and commitment to ophthalmology characterised by Dr Fehr'.

INGE FEHR

A year after she received her British citizenship, Inge married Dr Leopold Samson. Inge was twenty-six and Leopold (or Bimbo as he was known) was thirty-eight. The two had been introduced by a mutual friend and romance quickly followed.

Bimbo had also suffered under the Nazis. He had been the chief gynaecologist at the Hamburg Jewish Hospital at the young age of thirty-two. In November 1938 he was arrested and sent to Sachsenhausen concentration camp but was released following the intervention of the headmaster of Gordonstoun School, Kurt Hahn, who was his uncle and godfather. He was able to emigrate to Aberdeen, where he became a lecturer at the Medical School of Aberdeen University. After the fall of France, he was interned briefly in Canada. In 1945, he moved to Bishop's Stortford as gynaecologist at Herts and Essex Hospital.

Inge and Bimbo bought a large house right by the hospital so he could be available night and day as necessary. Bimbo delivered two of the couple's three boys.

Inge gave up nursing, devoting herself to the boys and spending any spare time entering slogan competitions. Despite English being her second language, she won 402 word-based competitions with prizes including a car,

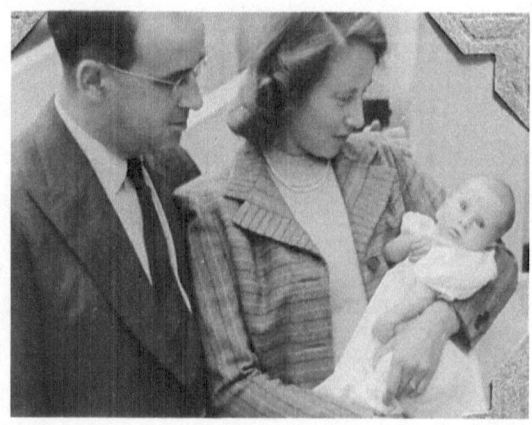

INGE AND BIMBO WITH THEIR FIRST CHILD, PETER

11.11.77 Bishop's Stortford Gazette

Inge — the woman with the Midas touch

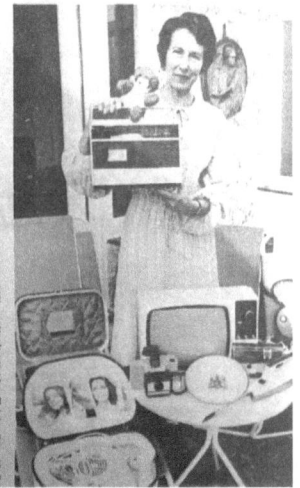

FATE, chance, fortune, skill — call it what you will. Lady Luck of Bishop's Stortford wins it all.

Perhaps this former refugee, Mrs Ingeborg Samson, has acquired a Cinderella "rags to riches" touch.

With earnest blue eyes, Inge (55) tells me half the joy of winning competition is sharing the prizes with her three sons.

"They provide useful birthday and Christmas presents", said Inge an ex-nurse. She's given her eldest son a honeymoon, while her latest prize, a spanking new caravan, will be for another son.

The caravan is ready for collection at Earls Court on November 14.

In 14 years she's won 383 prizes. A television, five watches, five holidays, silver, a barbecus, furniture, kitchen equipment, records, four radios, two cameras, and grocery vouchers. I could go on and on.

But Inge, a widow living in Warwick Road, remembers the strangest prize of all. A set of bongo drums.

"I did not know what to do with them", said Inge with her delightful German accent. "They were genuine, but oh so smelly. I gave them to one of my sons after living them a good clean", she said jovially.

That amazing lady goes hand

By Sandra Keetch

in hand.

She assures me the news of winning her 384th prize will be just as wonderful as the news of her first £5 prize for winning a soap powder competition.

Before 1963, Inge didn't know competitions existed. But a soap powder box entry form pushed through her letter-box began the craze.

Since then she's never looked back. This year she has won £3,000 worth of prizes.

"This is the best I have done. You learn by your mistakes and get to know what the judges look for," said Inge as she showed me a massive folder containing all the letters notifying her of wins.

"You must be original in your answers. And they must be apt to the product. Judges like humour, wit and rhyme." her book-case are her "bibles" — eight competition books giving hints on how to win. There is even a rhyming dictionary.

"This is useful for limericks," said Inge, who quite often things of winning phrases while queuing in the supermarket or gardening.

"Competitions are a relaxing and stimulating hobby. I do about 10 a month," said Inge.

"My big competition break came when I won a "Swinging London" beauty weekend at the Europa Hotel in 1969. For the first time I met other competitors and made good friends with whom I still correspond nearly every week," said Inge.

Swopping entry forms, and pooling knowledge and information she won more frequently.

Competition Journal lists the contests and Inge chooses which she will enter.

After hearing about the "London Competitors' Club" she became a member and in September became the "Dis-

---

OBSERVER
WON TWO HOLIDAYS IN THREE DAYS

IT has been a week to remember for Mrs Ingeborg Samson, of Warwick Road, Bishop's Stortford, for she heard within three days that she had won two holidays—prizes in two competitions she had entered.

Mrs Samson, who is a keen competition entrant, won a six-day holiday for two in France in the Bejam/Birds Eye Cookery Course Holiday Competition. The week will be spent attending the Dieppe cookery course under the guidance of a French chef, and of course there will be lots of sightseeing too.

She also won a seven-day holiday in Italy and £100 spending money in the Tartan World Competition.

"I could not believe it," said Mrs Samson, who is delighted about winning the two holidays.

She has been entering competitions since 1963 and she has won five holidays including the recent two and 374 other prizes which include a freezer and a washing machine.

Mrs Samson has lived in Bishop's Stortford since 1943 and she has three sons, Peter, Michael and John.

Mrs Samson has also just heard that she has won a plate to commemorate the Queen's Silver Jubilee in another competition she has entered.

INGE FEATURED IN LOCAL PAPERS *BISHOP'S STORTFORD GAZETTE* AND *BISHOP'S STORTFORD OBSERVER* IN 1978

IN HER LATER YEARS INGE TOOK HER SONS TO VISIT THE SITE OF HER OLD HOME IN BERLIN (PICTURED WITH SONS MICHAEL AND PETER - HER THIRD SON JOHN TOOK THE PHOTO)

AT THE LAUNCH OF THE FILM *THE RESCUERS* IN 2011 ABOUT THE WORK OF CAPTAIN FRANK FOLEY. BACK ROW LEFT TO RIGHT: INGE'S GRANDSON LEO AND SON MICHAEL. MIDDLE ROW: HELEN (ME), INGE'S GRANDDAUGHTER AMY AND SONS PETER AND JOHN. FRONT KITTY AND INGE

a caravan and multiple holidays, which she gave away as presents to her family. Inge's competition triumph was written about not only in the local press but even in *The Sunday Times Magazine* (8 October 1978).

Inge took great pride in the successes of her children. The eldest, Peter, was a senior executive at Microsoft, Michael was a science teacher and John a physics lecturer. She also had four grandchildren, Amelia, Matthew, Amy and Leo and three great-grandchildren.

Throughout her life, Inge spoke frequently about the injustices the family had suffered under the Nazis. She gave presentations regularly to schools stating 'these terrible things must never happen again'. The letters she received from children gave her great satisfaction. She contributed to several books and films, including *The Rescuers* (2011) about the heroic work of Captain Frank Foley and other diplomats during World War II.

Throughout her life she remained the best of friends with her sister Kitty.

Inge died on 19 December 2017 at the age of ninety-five.

KITTY FEHR

While Kitty had wanted to follow her father into medicine, these sought-after university places were reserved for returning servicemen. She opted instead for a course in chemistry and physiology at the University of London.

KITTY WITH ERNEST, 1960

WITH BABY HELEN (ME), 1963

DR KITTY GLANVILLE

After graduation, she started her career as a research chemist working in the pharmaceutical company Allen and Hanburys, which was subsequently absorbed into GSK. Every weekend she visited Oscar in his boarding house in Hampstead and paid regular visits to Inge and her growing family in Bishop's Stortford. As her father's health declined, Kitty took a greater role in his care.

Meanwhile she had started to date Ernest Glanville, a fellow resident at her father's boarding house. Ernest was a refugee from Vienna who prepared the boarding house's accounts in exchange for free board and lodging. The couple married in 1960, a year after Oscar's death.

In 1962 she gave birth to me, her only child. Kitty was a doting mother and although many women gave up work after having children at that time, she worked part-time as well as studying for a PhD.

Her employers were largely unsupportive. Kitty was asked to leave after she brought me into work one day when the nanny was sick. Having found a new laboratory and a new sponsor, Kitty was awarded a PhD in 1969.

Kitty stopped work in her forties to spend more time with her family. After Ernest's retirement in 1982, the couple travelled frequently and enjoyed playing bridge. She learnt fast and went on to win many trophies with Ernest. Kitty had two grandchildren, Freddie and Clara.

She died in August 2023, shortly before her hundredth birthday.

TIMELINE

March 1938
- Germany annexes Austria

August
- All Jews to add Israel or Sara to their names. Have to carry identity cards and passports stamped with J
— *Oscar banned from treating non Jews*

October
- Germany annexes Sudetenland

November
- Pogrom - Kristallnacht. Thousands of Jews taken into concentration camps
- Decree banning Jews from owning businesses
- Jews banned from cinemas, theatres or sports facilities
— *Oscar goes into hiding*
— *Fehrs approach Foley*

December
— *Fehr family visa to UK approved*

Jan 1939
- Hitler stated if war broke out would mean 'extermination' of European Jews.
- Jews banned from owning expensive jewellery or art
— *Fehrs surrender jewellery*

March
- Germany invades Czechoslovakia

April
— *Oscar receives working visa to UK*
— *SS takes over school building*

July
— *Jewish taxes paid. Passports returned*

August
— *Fehrs leave for UK*

September
- Germany invades Poland
- Britain and France declare war on Germany
- Hitler orders euthanasia of the disabled and mentally ill

November
- The USSR invades Finland

April 1940
- Germany invades Norway and Denmark
— *Family possessions sold by Nazis. Lose citizenship*

May
- Germany invades France, the Netherlands, Belgium, Luxembourg

June
— *Oscar interned. Released two months later*

July to October
- Battle of Britain - thwarting German invasion

September
- Start of the Blitz - Germany's bombing campaign kills at least 40,000 British civilians

April 1941
- Germany invades Yugoslavia and Greece

June
- Germany invades Soviet Union

September
- First gassings in Auschwitz

December
- US enters the war

January 1942
- 'Final Solution' agreed – extermination of European Jews
— *Oscar's sister and husband commit suicide. Another relative gassed. Toni, Oscar's first wife, and his brother-in-law are murdered by Nazis*

December
— *Jeanne dies*

May 1943
— *Oscar passes his exams and the family move to London*

July
— *Oscar starts work*

6 June 1944
- D Day. Allied forces land in Normandy

April 1945
- Hitler's suicide

May
- Germany surrenders

ACKNOWLEDGEMENTS

My thanks to my husband, Chris, and children, Freddie and Clara, for reading and re-reading versions of this text with great patience.

I am grateful for all the support from my cousins, Inge's boys; Peter, Michael and John, and from Peter's wife, Debra Lovio-Samson.

My thanks to my good friends Nicola Gibson, Jacqueline Kenney and Alison Hatherall for all their enthusiastic support and especially to Denise Bates for generously sharing her enormous industry experience and pointing me on the right track.

I was lucky to have a hugely capable team at Whitefox, especially Rosie Pearce, Jess King and the exceptional freelance copy-editor, Sadie Mayne.

On a different note, extraordinary gratitude must go to the late Captain Frank Foley, without whom our family story would have been so different.

NOTES

1. https://www.bbc.co.uk/bitesize/guides/z9y64j/revision/5#:~:text=TheWeimargovernment'smaincrisis,eventsthatincluded occupationC20hyperinflation
2. Smith, Michael, *Foley: The Spy who Saved 10,000 Jews* (London: 1999).
3. National Archives, reference 91/226/38, British Embassy, Berlin.
4. Heim, Steve J. (ed.), *Passages from Berlin: Recollections of former students and staff at the Goldschmidt Schule* (Maine: 1987).
5. Thompson, Gertrud H., *Dr Leonore Goldschmidt 1935–1941* (2005) https://leonoregoldschmidt.com/Lore1_21.pdf
6. Heim, Steve J. (ed.), *Passages from Berlin: Recollections of former students and staff at the Goldschmidt Schule* (Maine, 1987).
7. https://www.learningforjustice.org/classroom-resources/texts/the-reich-citzenship-law-of-september-15-1935
8. Smith, Michael, *Foley: The Spy who Saved 10,000 Jews* (London: 1999), p. 123.
9. https://ejewishphilanthropy.com/a-night-in-november-remembering-the-9th-of-november-1938-kristallnacht/
10. Smith, Michael, *Foley: The Spy who Saved 10,000 Jews* (London: 1999).
11. Smith, Michael, *Foley: The Spy who Saved 10,000 Jews* (London: 1999).
12. Pyke, D., 'Contributions by German émigrés to British medical science', *The Jewish Chronicle*, 8 September 2016.
13. Weisz, George M., 'The Medical Professional Elimination Program and the Ideology and Motivation of Nazi Physicians', *National Library of Medicine*, 28 October 2024, 15(4).

14 Heim, Steve J. (ed.), *Passages from Berlin: Recollections of former students and staff at the Goldschmidt Schule* (Maine, 1987).
15 National Archives CAB 23/75/27.
16 https://encyclopedia.ushmm.org/content/en/article/german-jewish-refugees-1933-1939
17 https://pmc.ncbi.nlm.nih.gov/articles/PMC4496449/
18 https://blog.nationalarchives.gov.uk/collar-lot-britains-policy-internment-second-world-war/
19 https://confidentials.com/manchester/warth-mills-the-bury-wwii-internment-camp-that-time-forgot
20 https://blog.nationalarchives.gov.uk/collar-lot-britains-policy-internment-second-world-war/
21 Dunera Boys, National Museum of Australia, https://www.nma.gov.au/defining-moments/resources/dunera-boys
22 https://beta.nationalarchives.gov.uk/explore-the-collection/stories/the-loss-of-ss-arandora-star/
23 https://confidentials.com/manchester/warth-mills-the-bury-wwii-internment-camp-that-time-forgot
24 https://static1.squarespace.com/static/5ed60e05b915bf68202571e3/t/623457ee355d6333622e6c3f/1647597552081/Hutchinson+Camp+Rollcall+v1.0.pdf
25 https://www.timesofisrael.com/as-holocaust-raged-uk-officials-blamed-jews-for-rising-wartime-anti-semitism/
26 https://hansard.parliament.uk/commons/1944-04-06/debates/1cfd5489-2c98-45d0-bf51-5a1c45669a18/PolishForcesGreatBritain(Anti-Semitism)
27 https://cupola.gettysburg.edu/cgi/viewcontent.cgi?article=1052&context=ghj
28 https://pmc.ncbi.nlm.nih.gov/articles/PMC4496449/
29 https://www.berlin.de/en/history/8481782-8619314-berlin-after-1945.en.html

ILLUSTRATION CREDITS

All photographs are personal family photographs except those detailed below:

p. 16: Library of Congress, George Grantham Bain Collection 1927

p. 17: Library of Congress, New York World-Telegram & Sun Collection

p. 18: Roger Rössing, Deutsche Fotothek

p. 31: IMAGO/Arkivi

p. 42: Scherl / Sueddeutsche Zeitung Photo / Alamy Stock Photo

p. 45: National Digital Archives

p. 54: John Bryant collection

p. 58: John Bryant collection

p. 59: Thomas Föhl

p. 67: Wiki Commons

p. 71: Wiki Commons

p. 74: German Federal Archives

P. 77 (top): Wiener Holocaust Library

p. 77 (bottom): John Bryant collection

p. 84: Wiki Commons

p. 101: Wiki Commons

p. 103 (top and bottom): Richard Fleischhut/NDL

p. 105: Scherl / Sueddeutsche Zeitung Photo / Alamy Stock Photo

p. 113: Wiki Commons

p. 128: Bury Council

p. 136: Mapa Scotland SCIO
p. 161: Ministry of Information Second World War Press Agency Print Collection, Imperial War Museum
p. 163: Landesarchiv Berlin

ABOUT THE AUTHOR

Helen John is the daughter of immigrants from Nazi Germany and Austria. Having graduated from a degree in history, she worked as a journalist, producer and TV director for the BBC, where she specialised in investigative programmes. For the past twenty years, Helen has worked as a media and presentation trainer.

She has two grown-up children, Freddie and Clara, and lives in London with her husband Chris.

www.ingramcontent.com/pod-product-compliance
Lightning Source LLC
Chambersburg PA
CBHW032106280426
43661CB00110B/1365/J